Advance praise f
Encounter with the I

Anika Pavel manages, from her present and sophisticated vantage, to evoke the innocence of youth. In pellucid prose she gives us both a history of transience – from Czechoslovakia to England – and the coming-of- age story of a brave young woman who travels open-eyed.

— **Nicholas Delbanco**, author,
most recently, of *Why Writing Matters*

Anika Pavel's essays have accomplished what we always ask of great writing, to transport us in place and time and original vision.
— **Mark Leichliter**, editor of bioStories Magazine.

This is a beautiful book, whose stories will long stay with you. Mesmerizing, evocative, and searching, it's a true pleasure to read.
— **Y. J. Fischer**

Encounter with the Future uses a series of interconnected essays to follow author Anika Pavel from her childhood in Iron Curtain Czechoslovakia to her struggles and then successes as an international fashion model and actor in mod era London to her present life as a writer, wife, mother and grandmother. The individual essays in story form chronicle this life still in forward motion, and are written with the wit and warmth and perceptiveness which characterize the author herself.

— **Kristopher Franklin**, author of *Silvercat*,
The High San Juan, *Relentless* and *Gravedigger*

Because Anika Pavel's life has been so remarkable, these fine essays often read like fiction. Displaced but never untethered, Anika Pavel offers consistent clear-eyed vision steeped in compassion and grace, refusing the preconceptions others might place on her refugee status.

— **Mark Hummel**, author of Man, Underground

The stories in this collection bring vividly to life a time, a place, a family, and a unique perspective. The reader learns about Communist Czechoslovakia and London in the swinging 60s - not just historical events and figures, but the texture of daily life. In a voice that contains all the layers of naivete and wisdom that have accrued over the years, Anika Pavel tells us stories that are at turns funny and poignant, sometimes at the same time, and always memorable.

— **Emma Hamilton**, Professor of Literature

"A beautifully written and captivating memoir that will make you look differently at your own life."

— **Cindi Myers**, author of, most recently, *Mile High Mystery*

"Each narrative is a testament to the resilience of the human spirit, offering glimpses of hope, resilience, and the enduring capacity for love and laughter in the face of adversity."

— **Martina Moravcova**, the Slovak Olympic medalist

encounter

with

the

future

anika pavel

CASTLE
PUBLISHING

ISBN: 979-8-9902316-0-3 (paperback)
ISBN: 979-8-9902316-1-0 (ebook)

Library of Congress Control Number: 2024900302

Every effort has been made to trace or contact all copyright
holders. The publishers will be pleased to make good any
omissions or rectify any mistakes brought to their attention
at the earliest opportunity.

Many people I mentioned in this book have long since passed
away. But those that are or should be still alive, I have asked if
they would prefer, I give them a fictional name or use their own.
Most opted for their own name. Those whom I was unable to
contact, I did give a fictional name.

Book design and typesetting by InsideStudio26.com.

First printing edition 2024.

Castle Publishing
castel.publishing.information@gmail.com

To my Parents

I would like to dedicate this book to my father, Jan Kocvara who grew up during two world wars, yet remained an optimist who believed in human kindness. My mother, Emilia Kocvarova, believed in the power of books. She believed that knowledge was the remedy to all of the world's problems.

contents

freedom

When I opened my eyes, I did not recognize the sun-soaked room. Then it came to me. I was in my dream. Not dreaming a dream. I was living the dream. I was in England. Flesh and blood, body and soul.

My attic room was not quite *Jane Eyre*, but to me, it was special. The window was small, and too high for me to be able to see out of, but, on a sunny day, the little square filled the room with bright light.

I looked at my watch. It was 9:00 a.m. My stomach reminded me that it had not received any food since my lunch at the Prague airport in Communist Czechoslovakia some twenty hours earlier.

I had just turned eighteen and was embarking on a journey to the unknown. My father, who was a tailor, made me new trousers and a flannel shirt before I left home. It was the middle of November, so I put on the sweater my mother knitted for me.

"Wear it when you need strength," she said. "The sweater will not give you wisdom, that has to come from you, but it will comfort you." She wiped her tears and added, "Each stitch has part of my heart in it." It was my mother's trademark to be wise and dramatic at the same time.

I unpacked and organized my clothing. I straightened the bed. Making my hands busy did not, however, silence my stomach, or change the reality that I had to face people in the house. I practiced the words aloud one more time. "Good morning. My name is Jarmila. I am the new au pair." I was sure I would find some dishes in the kitchen, wash them, and then ask for food. I was too hungry to allow the scenario of no dirty dishes as a possibility.

Slowly I descended the two flights of stairs holding my breath and hoping none of the stairs would creak. I was not ready to hold an unscripted conversation. I made it to the kitchen and to my relief it was empty of people but not dirty dishes.

"Good morning. I am Scott. You must be the new au pair." To my delight, I understood the tall young man who had just entered the kitchen. He smiled. I smiled back. But my relief did not last long. When he spoke again, I was unable to follow his questions. Scott noticed my panic-stricken face and walked over to the refrigerator. He took out an egg and showed it to me. "An egg," he said. I smiled nervously. He asked a few more questions, but soon he concluded that it was fair to leave the culinary decision about my egg to him. As of that morning, I would recognize the words *egg, toast, butter* and *tea* in any conversation.

Mrs. Landis, the woman I was going to work for, came in as I was finishing my tea. She had a round, motherly figure and was not very tall. Her hair was dark, curly, and cut very short. As time went by, she would tell me with some regularity that she needed to go on a diet. She followed the proclamation with a wink and warm smile.

With the help of a dictionary and a lot of show and point, Mrs. Landis explained what she expected of me.

I already knew from my Slovak friend Ondrej, who picked me up at Heathrow airport, that Mrs. Landis's children were grown and out of the house.

Ondrej was the son of my mother's coworker in Czechoslovakia. It was through my mom's friendship with Ondrej's mother that she learned about the job in Ipswich, England. Mrs. Landis rented rooms in her house and Ondrej briefly stayed in her house after he made his daring escape from then-"iron-locked" Czechoslovakia. It was there that the idea of an au pair job was created.

At the time of my arrival, Mrs. Landis had four lodgers for whom I was to cook dinners. Everybody, including Mrs. Landis, was responsible to keep his or her bedroom clean. My job was to keep the kitchen, dining room, hallways, stairs, and bathrooms clean, as well as Mrs. Landis's living room, which I was invited to use even when she was using it herself. This was a privilege not extended to the lodgers. The house had only two bathrooms. The smaller bathroom was on the ground floor, just outside of Mrs. Landis's bedroom, and it was for her exclusive use. The larger bathroom, which was to be used by the rest of the occupants of the house, was located on the second floor.

Mrs. Landis also had an office/examination room, which she asked me to vacuum occasionally, but mostly she kept that room clean herself. I knew that the work description of an au pair, which normally involved caring for young children, did not really apply, but I was brought up to respect work, any work, and I was grateful for the opportunity to come to England.

In addition to being a retired emergency nurse, Mrs. Landis was also licensed to practice natural medicine. Later, when my English was much improved, she told me how she became interested in alternative medicine.

Her husband worked in a rural hospital in Rhodesia (now Zimbabwe) and she was his nurse.

"There were times he was away helping in rural villages and he was gone for days, even weeks. I was left to fend for myself, and for people who needed help." She spoke about the hardship of the local population, but specifically the women. "I could never forget the suffering of those women…and girls…I did what I could, but it was mostly only temporary."

Her face reflected painful memories that would not fade.

"But the women showed me how, using the local herbs, they eased their own pain and the pain of their children." I had the impression that part of her was still in Africa.

"So, now I hope to help women here," she said more cheerfully.

The lodgers did their best to help me learn English. Mr. Brodie was older, probably in his fifties, a father figure to us all. Even when my English got much better, I had a hard time understanding him. "Ayah, that's because I am Scottish," he told me when I asked him to repeat what he just said.

Fred was a laborer and he kept a parakeet in his room. I could hear the bird chirping every time I passed his room. He was short, stocky, and I remember his hands had a lot of calluses on them. He had a cockney accent but he tried very hard to speak "proper" so that I could understand him.

Ernest was quiet and occasionally smoked a pipe. He was an engineer and I stayed in touch with him the longest.

Scott, who made my first breakfast, was an accountant and had a pretty girlfriend whom he visited on weekends.

Mrs. Landis's friend Roy stayed in the largest bedroom in the house. There was gossip among the lodgers that Mrs. Landis often stayed overnight in his bedroom.

I settled into a pattern of cleaning, cooking, and listening to Pirate Radio Caroline, which was stationed on a ship in the international waters not far from the East Anglia coast. It was established to circumvent the record companies and the monopoly of the BBC radio broadcast. The outlandish DJs kept me happy playing the latest pop music.

Within a few months, I could read books and converse on many topics. When Mrs. Landis had no patients, she liked to stop by the kitchen and talk to me. She would make me lunch, usually a salad. In Czechoslovakia we did not eat salad as a main course so at first, I was waiting for my real meal. But soon I learned to like those salads and even looked forward to them.

While we ate, she told me that her family came to England from Russia shortly after the Russian Revolution, but she knew very little about their life. Most of the adults died of some virus soon after they came to England, leaving behind orphans and questions about their history. While I washed the dishes, she would ask me what I thought about life in England and the escalation of the American war in Vietnam. Was it really worth the fight to stop Communism from spreading? How bad was life in a Communist country?

In my still-limited English, I explained that the widespread shortages in Czechoslovakia were the result of central planning as much as party cronyism, resulting in incompetent people running the country. Sometimes it would be butter, other times toilet paper, that was hard to get.

My mother would go shopping with a bottle of Slivovica or a piece of material my father managed to save if she did not want to come home empty-handed. You bought whatever was available and then decided what you could make out of it. Thanks to my mother's ability to stretch a meager piece of meat to several meals and with the magic of the herbs always in pots in the windows, she made it taste delicious. My father's genius to cut garments in the way that would guarantee leftover material for his children was a skill that kept us all reasonably well dressed. Anti-Soviet jokes were whispered and nobody believed anything published in the papers.

There were some positive aspects of a child's life in a Communist country. All artistic talents were encouraged and free to participate in. Sports, too, were free, and I did take full advantage of that benefit. Emancipation of women was a norm. From the fourth grade to eighth grade, once a week we had domestic study. For two hours, usually on Monday, the boys and girls learned to sew, embroider, knit, mend, etc. On Friday, for two hours, we learned how to use a hammer, saw, screwdriver, nails, screws, and later how to mend simple breakages, hang a curtain, etc. This simple "handyman" education would prove to be very useful to me.

But the political aspects were harder to judge. I did not know how much of what I was taught was true and what was propaganda. I had nothing to compare it to.

My father's perspective, however, was molded by hardship. He was born into a peasant family during the Austro-Hungarian Empire. The Hungarians were particularly ruthless in their enslavement of the Slovak people. After WWI the Treaty of Versailles freed the Czechs and Slovaks from the rule of Germans, Austrians, and Hungarians. While Tomas Garrick Masaryk fought internationally to secure the first Czech-Slovak republic, ultimately it was due to the Allies' desire to create a buffer between them and the looming threat of Soviet Russia that played the decisive role in creating the first Czechoslovak Republic, which came to be on October 28, 1918.

The new republic did provide my father the chance to learn a profession. Through hard work he built a successful tailor shop and wrote an instructional book on tailoring.

WWII threatened my father's life and his business, but it was the Communists who came after the war who confiscated his shop. He was labeled "petty bourgeois" and threatened with prison. At the age of fourteen, my older brother Jan had to wash dishes for one year in a local hotel "to get closer to the proletariat" before he was allowed to enroll in high school. By the time I was my brother's age, that requirement was dropped. My father bitterly resented that his son was punished for his success.

My father's first wife died of an aneurysm. I never asked, but sometimes wondered, knowing how much my father wanted children, if that desire had played a role in choosing a second wife eighteen years his junior.

My mother was born into abject poverty, but her craving was not for food but for knowledge. But she did not get attracted to the Communist ideals, instead, she focused on getting an education. She never forgot her inability to go to school due to the lack of shoes. Her family had only one pair of boots between five children. The two-room school was a good three kilometers away, so, in winter it meant that only one child could go to school.

Her oldest brother, Martin, left for America when my mother was a young girl. Imagining his life in a foreign country was the start of her lifelong desire to travel. "Travel is the University of Life," she would tell us, often. So, it was not surprising that she seized the first opportunity to open the door to the world for me. She wanted me to experience the life she could only dream about.

In January 1968, Alexander Dubcek was elected the First Secretary and established a free press and the freedom to travel. I did not know it at the time, but I was an early benefactor of the loosening of the Soviet yoke. I told Mrs. Landis how more than anything else in the world, I wanted to make my mother's dream to travel a reality. Without hesitation, she invited both my parents to come and stay with her in Ipswich.

I wanted to earn Mrs. Landis's generosity. I offered to help with her patients. Mrs. Landis explained that sometimes she performed small surgeries and some patients liked to stay overnight. "So, yes, you can help."

Not a suspicious person by nature, I did not notice that those who stayed overnight were all young girls. When I would find a girl crying, huddled in a blanket on the sofa in the living room, my primary concern was to make her comfortable. I would tell funny stories about how my brothers and I got into trouble stealing cherries from the neighbor's garden, while our family was famous in the neighborhood for having the best cherry tree right in our yard.

My favorite story to tell was about my brother who was a huge James Fenimore Cooper fan and knew *The Last of the Mohicans* by heart. One day when he was about eleven years old, and I was nine, my brother told me he would demonstrate to me the art of scalping. He explained in gruesome detail how the Indians would scalp their enemy. Horrified, I started to scream. My mother and the incredible volume of my voice rescued me. However, when my mother inspected my brother's pockets, the most sinister item she found was a black pencil.

Mrs. Landis said I would make a good nurse, and I liked the idea, but after she included the task of emptying the bedpan, I changed my mind. I did not like the sight of blood and I flushed it down the toilet fast.

The weeks passed and spring arrived with its usual fanfare. The days became warmer and longer. The famous English gardens began to resemble the beauty the poets wrote about with so much eloquence, but I was blind to it all. I was focused on the day I would embrace my parents.

At last, the day I imagined so many times had arrived. True to our Slovak emotions, we hung on to each other and cried happy tears. And then, my mother opened her suitcase. It was, as I knew it would be, full of my favorite cookies, lovingly baked by her. The sweet aroma of the *kolach* hit my nose, and in a box wrapped with particular care was my favorite, the *strudel.*

It was late when I showed my parents how to sleep in a bed without a duvet. The secret to comfort, I told them, is to pull out the top sheet and the blankets that were firmly tucked under the mattress so that the feet could get unrestricted movement. I closed the door and smiled at the thought of putting my parents to bed.

Refreshed after a good night's sleep, we were ready to embark on some serious sightseeing. I took my parents to the nearby seaside town of Felixstowe. Like all people from landlocked countries, the first thing my parents wanted to do was taste the water in the ocean. Is it really salty? Next, I introduced them

In Felixstowe... is the ocean really salty?

to fish and chips. My father joked that he had never had anything so good that came out of the newspaper. He was referencing the distaste he felt toward anything he read in newspapers like *Pravda* (which ironically means "truth" in both Slovak and Russian).

For my mother, the visit to Cambridge was akin to a devout Catholic going to the Vatican. Because she had only a scant education and was essentially self-taught, the walk through the buildings that in her mind were a bastion of knowledge was immensely important to her. While we sat in the Kings College Chapel, my mother told me that parts of her feet were still numb from the frostbites she suffered walking to school when it was too far into winter. Later, walking on one of the many courtyards' impeccably maintained grass lawns, she took off her shoes and walked barefoot on the soft, cooling grass. I hoped that the softness of the grass might soothe the pain in her feet.

The freedom to travel was intoxicating. I had never seen my parents look so happy. Walking on the beach at Felixstowe, I watched them breathe in the salty air as if they were storing it for years to come.

After a pleasant day, we were sitting in the kitchen when Mrs. Landis came in and asked me to follow her to the living room. She stopped in front of the closed living room door. I could hear the TV. She was searching for words, but finally just opened the door.

"I am so very sorry," she said.

My eyes fell on the TV screen. Tanks filled Prague's Wenceslas Square. They were pointing at the city and people were lying in front of them. Bloodied young people screamed, "Go home" in Czech. Many had climbed the statue of St. Wenceslas, waving a torn and bloodied Czechoslovakian flag. Like thieves, during the night of August 20-21, airplanes full of tanks and artillery landed at Ruzyne Airport and took over Prague while the nation slept.

Together with St. Wenceslas, I looked on the carnage below. I heard the words "end to Prague Spring" coming from the TV but for a moment I could not process them. I stood shocked, suspended between disbelief and reality. The door opened and my parents stood in the doorway looking at the TV screen.

My head moved from the TV to my parents in an involuntary motion. My father's slight body reflected hundreds of hours spent bent over his sewing machine. The wrinkles on his kind face deepened in sorrow. He sat on a chair and put his hands on his knees. I could not tell if his hands were keeping his legs steady or was it the other way around, but it was the resignation in his gray eyes that I could not bear. He had allowed himself to believe in the possibility of freedom and once again he had to watch the hope trampled under the might of tanks and the power behind them.

My mother's hands held each other but she could not stop them from trembling. "What are we going to do?" she asked. My father sat next to his wife holding her in silence.

Dubcek and five of his colleagues were abducted and taken to an unknown location in the Soviet Union. The president of Czechoslovakia, Ludvik Svoboda, a highly respected war general decorated by the Soviet Union, went to Moscow for negotiations. He knew that if he did not bring Dubcek back to Prague, with the troops already in the country, there would be a bloodbath.

The week following the invasion was filled with chaos. My brother Pavel was the only member of our family still in Czechoslovakia. My older brother Jan was in Wales. He studied English and his university had arranged a summer program at Cardiff University.

Pavel called us on the telephone.

"I can get to Vienna and from there to England," he said, breathless. "Austria is letting people in and the Slovak guards are letting people through. What should I do?"

I looked at my father. The decision had to be made on the spot. After a long pause my father said: "Tell him to stay." His voice was heavy, as if delivering the verdict of a life sentence without parole. I relayed my father's words and asked my brother to call again if he could.

We sat in deafening silence, each deep in our own contemplation. I could not get my brother Pavel out of my mind. After my mother went to bed, I asked my father,

"Why did you tell him to stay?"

"Your mother is battling cancer," he said. "I am eighteen years older than she is. Did you think I would put an albatross like that on your neck?"

I knew there was no point in arguing. We said good night, both hiding our tears.

After my parents returned home, Mrs. Landis told me that if I wanted, I could stay and work for her. After the Invasion, Britain gave all Czechoslovak citizens living in England a work permit and the permission to stay indefinitely. My mother's health was holding up, giving me the time to weigh my options.

Absorbed by my own challenges, I paid little attention to Mrs. Landis and her activities. Any questions about the girls who stayed in the house were part of my usual lack of suspicion.

Finally, I came to my decision. I would take Mrs. Landis's offer to stay and work for her during the day, and take evening classes to study English and history so that I could learn what kind of lies I'd been fed by the Communist schooling.

I asked Mrs. Landis if I could talk to her.

"I have to talk to you, too," she said, gesturing for me to sit. "Things have changed in the past few weeks and I may have to sell the house." She paused. "That is not all."

Being preoccupied herself, she was unaware that I had spent the previous few weeks in my own shattered universe, picking up the pieces and putting them together like a wounded jigsaw puzzle.

"There is a good chance that I will go to prison," she said. I was sure I misunderstood. In my mind I searched for a word that would sound like *prison*.

"Did you hear me, dear?" she asked.

"Did you say prison?" I asked.

"Yes. Prison," she reiterated, looking at me.

"Why?" I asked.

"You don't know?" She paused, scrutinizing my face. "You really don't know, do you?" She sounded half amused.

"Did I do something wrong?" I asked.

"No. Nothing you did," she said. She explained that some of the small surgeries she performed had in fact terminated pregnancies. Although abortion in England was made legal the year before, it was frowned upon by doctors and nurses and was generally hard to obtain.

"In Rhodesia I terminated early pregnancy for women who already had too many children who were hungry," she said.

After she got her license to practice alternative medicine, Mrs. Landis had built up a small clientele.

"A patient I had treated for eczema earlier came back begging for help. She was pregnant. She was seventeen years old, frightened and desperate. The hospital would inform her parents, so she could not go there. I spoke to her about responsibility and told her if she got into trouble again, I would tell her parents myself. But..., in the end I terminated her pregnancy." She put her head in her hands and breathed heavily.

"After that, girls were making appointments for a dermatology consultation, but what they wanted was an abortion."

I was stunned. Suddenly, the girls' cries, the pain, it was all making sense. How could I have been so stupid?

"One of the girls was too far along, and I refused to terminate her pregnancy. She was angry and reported me."

"Did I...?" I was unable to verbalize the question to which, I suddenly was pretty sure, I knew the answer.

"They were all very, very early," she said. "You must not blame yourself."

"I don't," I said, and left the room.

I threw myself on the bed. The jigsaw puzzle that I had constructed so carefully had crumbled, and some pieces I would never recapture.

The memory of the young girls would not leave me. Their faces reflected happy relief as they gave me small tokens of thanks. I threw them all into the garbage, but that did nothing to reconcile my head and my heart.

Was it because I felt duped into doing something I did not know that I was doing? But if I were told, and asked to help, would I have refused?

The next morning Mrs. Landis told me that her solicitor wanted to talk to me and perhaps sign some papers if need be. She said she would pay for my train ticket.

"Where is his office?" I asked.

"London."

I decided I would go to London, but I would not come back to Ipswich. I had a few pounds saved, and I would find a job.

The next day I stood with Mrs. Landis on a railway platform, each of us absorbed in our own guilt.

"I asked Mr. Frost to secure a room for you at the YWCA for the first few nights." Mrs. Landis tried to sound matter-of-fact. "You know you can come back, tonight, or any time." She was fighting tears.

"Yes," was all I managed without bursting into tears. I felt I was betraying her. I knew she was a good woman.

When the train pulled out of the station, I waved to the lone figure on the platform, and then she was gone.

I remembered how to navigate London from the happier times when I visited with my parents. By the time I reached Great Marlborough Street, I felt empowered by the city. I walked into the office of Claude Hornby and Frost with confidence, which promptly disappeared when I was told that Mr. Frost was delayed in court, and would I please come back tomorrow at 10:00 a.m.? And no, there wasn't any message for me.

The office was on the corner of Great Marlborough Street and Carnaby Street. I walked down Carnaby Street, full of boutiques like Mary Quant, Lord John, and Mary Jane, where it was not unusual to spot a pop star shopping. The music coming from the "fab" shops was loud and for the moment the voices of the Beatles, Kinks, Small Faces, Bee Gees, overpowered the panic that threatened to overtake me.

I kept walking until I found myself at Piccadilly Circus, which was full of people. I no longer felt alone; I was part of the crowd, one of many. Loneliness was not possible in the flowing humanity that surrounded me. I sat on the edge of the fountain and watched people rushing about. One day I knew it would be me. I will have a place to go from, and a place to go to. It was up to me to find both.

I started to walk toward Victoria Station. It held the memory of my parents. I found the bench where the three of us sat, talked, cried, and finally said goodbye.

I walked over to a telephone booth that had a promising number of directories. I started to look for the YWCA hostels and their addresses and telephone numbers. I made several calls to the nearby hostels that I hoped I could afford, but they were all full for the night.

I realized it was getting late. I noticed a policeman telling a couple of people who were sleeping on the benches to move along. I watched an old man who carried his entire belongings with him lift himself up with difficulty from a hard bench and slowly move across the station and out into the dark city. I pretended to talk into the phone's receiver; I did not want to be told to leave. For a second, I wondered if I had missed the last train to Ipswich.

I looked around and found the least conspicuous phone booth. I had an apple and a piece of cheese in my handbag. I cleaned the apple on my shirt and slowly ate it with the cheese. Then I created a kind of chair out of my suitcase, my canvas bag, and my handbag. My mother's sweater served as a pillow.

I slept in short snatches of time. Finally, it was light again and the station hummed with its early morning ritual. Strangely, I did not feel tired. I was invigorated by the prospect of the new day and the new beginning. I untangled my leg from the corner of the booth.

The bathrooms were open, and I did the best I could with my limited resources. I sat on my parents' bench until it was time to start my own walk toward the offices of Claude Hornby and Frost.

* * *

I sat in a brown leather chair facing an enormous desk. Mr. Frost stood behind the desk and looked at me with kind eyes. He asked me where I was staying, but then he interrupted himself before I had a chance to speak.

"Heavens, I forgot about you yesterday. I was held up in court. I trust you managed." His question made my night in the telephone booth real, and I struggled not to cry.

After I answered all the legal questions relating to Mrs. Landis's case, Mr. Frost offered me a job as a receptionist in his office. I would be paid ten pounds a week, which made me feel very rich. I was getting three pounds a week up to then, courtesy of Mrs. Landis.

I stepped out of the office, and I was back on Carnaby Street. Since I did not have to look for a job anymore, I allowed myself an hour to savor the atmosphere of pop culture and let my dreams run free. To the tunes of Cliff Richard, I pictured spending my entire week's salary at least three times over in what quickly became my favorite boutique, called Mary Jane.

In the last shop on my tour of mental indulgence, I noticed a black-and-white poster of Alexander Dubcek. His face filled the poster. Below his face in large red letters was one word. FREEDOM. In his expression was the pain of the nation. I stood transfixed, unable to move.

Finally, a Robin Gibb lookalike came over and asked me if I wanted to buy the poster. I explained why I would like to buy it, and why I could not spare the money. To my surprise, he wrapped up the poster and gave it to me. I was touched by his kindness, but the fact that he knew who Dubcek was, was even more important to me. I would pay him back from my first paycheck.

By seven that evening, I was having dinner at a YWCA that I found in the Yellow Pages. It was in Archway; I would share a bedroom with two other girls and I would get breakfast and dinner Monday to Friday. On weekends, I would get lunch. This would cost me three pounds, seventeen shillings, and sixpence. By the time I would pay for the Underground and my lunch, there was not much left.

I fell in love with London. From my perch in the office of Claude Hornby and Frost, I watched Paul McCartney go into Great Marlborough Court to marry Linda Eastman. Joe Cocker revolutionized the Beatles' song "With a Little Help from My Friends," and people in the office adopted me. I was very happy.

One day Mr. Frost called me to his office.

"I had a letter from Mrs. Landis," he said. "She asked if you would come and visit her." He gave me the address, date, and the time when I could go and visit. I calculated that the trip would wipe out almost all my savings, but I knew I would go.

It was a gloomy winter Sunday and I wondered what the prison would be like. I pictured every prison I had ever seen in movies. To my surprise, the prison was a converted old English manor house. The gentry who owned the house owed back taxes and the solicitors worked out a deal in which the government got lumbered with the drafty house. Not inclined to spend money on the old place, the government had made it into a prison for women.

Mrs. Landis was serving an eighteen-month sentence for performing abortions. We sat in a large vestibule that had clearly witnessed grandeur in its past. Everyone talked in hushed tones, as if it were some posh hotel lobby that had fallen on hard times, but the clientele had retained its dignity by solemn behavior.

Mrs. Landis encouraged me to stay in England. "It will get worse back in your homeland," she said, "and you can help your family more from here than if you go back and subject yourself to who knows what trumped-up charges." She grilled me about my work, and if I had a boyfriend.

"I decided not to sell the house," she announced. "Feel free to visit there anytime you want; I've decided to go to Israel for a year or two after I come out."

She kept changing subjects. We talked about everything except the elephant in the room. I promised to come again.

It was dark by the time I boarded the train for the long journey back. I pondered the notion—whether to go home or stay. Could I live without the freedom I had grown accustomed to? Could I really be in danger if I returned? But, ultimately, there was only one question that mattered. Was I prepared to become an immigrant?

I closed my eyes and thought about the non-conversation that took place between Mrs. Landis and me. I searched my mind and my soul as to what, if anything, I would do differently if I knew that the girls staying with Mrs. Landis were there to have abortions. I tried to picture myself in the shoes of those girls.

What would I do? Right now, at this moment, I could barely take care of myself. I had nobody to lean on, and I knew that at any moment my family might need to lean on me.

For a while my mind played ping-pong between two daunting conundrums. Eventually, I was rescued by fatigue and the monotonous sound of the train. I fell into drowsy semi-consciousness.

Out of the fog emerged the figure of Mrs. Landis, the unlikely women's "libber," who had no desire to burn her bra, but who would help women at the risk of going to prison. Who was I to judge?

Freedom appeared in the Spring 21 issue of *Tint Journal*. (*Tint Journal* is open exclusively to writers for whom English is a second language.)

lost and found

"Why are you crying?"
   "I lost my mother," sobbed a little girl.
   "Do you know your name?" asked the man.
   "Yes."
   "Can you tell me?"
   "Yes."
   "What is it?"
   "My name is Jarmila Kocvarova."

No amount of secular push to replace Christmas with some feeble winter celebration could dilute the spirit and excitement of Christmas for children in Communist-controlled countries in central Europe. The splendor of Christmas could be seen in every family window, and even the shops were decorated to the nines.

After all, even Communists needed to sell merchandise, such as it was.

I was born in a country that sadly no longer exists. I think of Czechoslovakia as the Little Big Nation, geographically small but big in its history and its people.

My story began in a town called Trnava, which was located in the second half of Czecho-Slovakia. It was called Little Rome or a Slovak Rome. The town was home to 30,000 inhabitants, eleven Catholic churches, two monasteries, and a convent. The wall and the moat, built in the thirteenth century to ward off invaders, still surround the old town.

Despite Trnava's impressive history, when I was a little girl, my focus was on the main street. Specifically on a very large store that sold all sorts of merchandise that even my imagination failed to invent. The name of the store was easy to remember. It was called ASO, an early version of a department store. (It is still there, unchanged.)

The old town stood proudly in its Christmas garb; the lights winked merrily at passersby and people's whispers were just a bit louder than usual. Having nothing to compare it to, as a child I thought it was all very beautiful. In retrospect, the simple beauty that did not get drowned in overabundance I would get used to later; it really was beautiful.

I was little more than three years old when my mother took me with her to buy baking pans at the big store in town. Christmas was not far off and my mother wanted to start making the Christmas cookies ready for offering everyone that came to the house during the second half of December and first half of January.

Unfortunately for my mother, the toy department at ASO, the departments store, was just before the baking supplies department. As we were making our way toward my mother's destination, I spotted a doll that the only other girl in our neighborhood had, and who would not let me play with it. When, unexpectedly, I was presented with a chance to get the doll, I stood transfixed and I would not move from the counter displaying the doll.

My mother did her best to lure me away, saying if I'd go with her so she could buy what she came for, I might find the doll under the Christmas tree. But Christmas was more than two weeks away and to a three-year-old girl, even a week seemed like an eternity. I was determined to get the doll then and there while it was physically within my reach.

My mother decided to wait me out. The patience of a busy mother, however, could not compete with a child standing close to her prize. From her stance between the toy department and the baking department, my mother could see what she needed to buy, and after a while she decided she could buy what she needed while keeping her eye on me. But little people can disappear remarkably fast.

Meanwhile, I was being pushed by the crowed of people all trying to get closer to the counter so they could get the server's attention. A big woman obstructed my vision for just a little while and when she moved, I could not see my mother. I moved left, then right but I still could not see her.

Suddenly the crowd of shoppers who bought what they came for were moving toward the door and swept me away from the doll and my mother. I found myself outside the store where people went in different directions, and I suddenly stood alone without my mother. I started to cry. A few people looked at me but assumed a child wanted something the parent did not want to buy for her. Not an unusual situation for that time of the year.

After a while the man who first passed me like the others came back and asked, "Why are you crying?"

"I lost my mother," I said, sobbing.

"Where did you lose your mother?"

"There." I pointed at the crowded store.

"What is your name?"

"Jarmila."

"Do you know your second name?"

"Jarmila Kocvarova."

"Do you know where you live?"

"Spiegelsalle," I said and stopped crying.

"Do you remember the name of the street?" he asked. I shook my head.

"All right, we will go to Spiegelsalle and see if we can find your home."

The man held my hand as we passed the wall that separated the town from Spiegelsalle.

In the past, Jewish people were not allowed to live inside the wall of the town. The noblemen, however, did business with Jews, who became very prosperous. They built large homes with halls decorated by ornate mirrors (Spiegel - glass, Salle - hall in Yiddish).

By WWI, Spiegelsalle was occupied by people of all religions, but the name remained.

The man did not ask me any more questions and we walked in silence. After a while we came to a corner where I turned right.

"Why did you turn?" asked the man.

"We always go this way."

The man smiled, realizing that instinctively I knew the way home. Soon we were ringing the doorbell on my house.

It was dark and my father did not see me right away.

"What am I making for you?" he asked, thinking the man came to collect something he made for him.

"I found your daughter crying in front of ASO and brought her home."

"Where is her mother?" asked my father.

The two men looked at each other. The confusion was mutual.

"Come in and have some wine." My father recovered, inviting the man more in the hope he would shed some light on the puzzling situation than out of politeness.

"I wish I could but I am in a hurry." The man shook my father's hand and walked away.

"Where is your mother?" My father looked at me and I started to cry.

He took me inside and handed me to my grandmother. While she got me ready for bed, my father filled her in with what little he knew. I waited for my father to get angry with me, but instead both my father and grandmother Katarina hugged me more than usual. I knew that when my mother comes, I will be in trouble, so I was more than willing to go to bed.

Although tired, I was too frightened to sleep. I lay in the bed with my eyes closed waiting for my punishment. The doll that had caused all the problems lost its luster.

"No, don't wake her up now," I heard my father whisper. I lay still under warm blankets with my eyes firmly closed, petrified.

"Please let me see her," sobbed my mother.

"Well, I will be going back to the station now that all is well."

I heard a man's voice but I did not dare to open my eyes to see who he was.

The door to the bedroom closed and for a while I listen to the muted voices of my parents and my grandmother. I began to feel guilty for making my mother cry.

"What happened to you?" whispered my brother Jan. My closed eyes did not fool him.

"Did you run away?" My brother Pavel wanted some drama.

"No," I whispered back. "I got lost."

"How?" My brothers demanded details but got disappointed that the man who brought me home was boring and ordinary. Nonetheless, my brothers relished telling me, "Oh wow, you will get punished tomorrow."

While I had been walking home with the kind stranger, my mother went to the police station hoping someone had brought me there. Seeing her on the verge of panic, one of the policemen went with her to ASO to ask people, mostly the employees, if they have seen a little girl wandering about alone. Drawing no positive results and because there were no telephones, the policeman suggested checking to see if I might have found my way home.

In the morning my mother explained the best way she could to a three-year-old how much worry my behavior caused her. To my brother's disappointment, the only punishment I received was that I had to learn our address, and worse (in my brother's opinion), I did get that doll for Christmas!

My mother would mention the incident from time to time, always regretting she could not thank the kind man personally. Later, when I was older, I became aware how my mother helped strangers, some of whom became friends. It was her way of thanking the person she would never meet.

For many years I did not understand the terror I put my mother through. But after I had my own children, any time we went shopping, they would get anything they wanted out of me even past the time when they could safely make their way home alone.

mind over matter

I kept my eyes on the dark, icy pavement while I hung on to my mother's hand for fear of being blown away. The wind twisted in the narrow passage of the crossroad and threatened to freeze my already-cold limbs. We were walking home from my school where my third-grade class had celebrated Father Frost and the upcoming New Year. In Communist Czechoslovakia the school walls were decorated with pictures, not of Santa Claus, but of an old white man covered in dots of snow wearing a funny hat. He was feeding squirrels and birds while children were skating or building a snowman.

Not many of the streetlights were lit but those that were helped to cast a long shadow on the pavement as we made our way home. My mother and I had left the winter wonderland of my classroom and now watched the wind tossing the dust and small debris into a whirlpool of air.

"I wish it would snow," said my mother.

"Why?" I asked.

"Because after it snows, it always warms up."

My breath reminded me of the white clouds spewing out of a locomotive's funnel as it pulled out of the railway station. I could feel the wind penetrating the fabric of my winter coat, under which there was nothing more than my snowflake dress that looked fancy on the school stage but outside on a cold street was woefully inadequate.

We were halfway home when I started to cry. My face felt frozen solid, I told my mother. She took off her scarf and wrapped it around my head so that only my eyes were visible.

"We will walk ten steps and then run ten steps. It will make us warmer and get us home faster, but most importantly we have to rebuff the cold."

"How?" I asked.

"We refuse to be cold. Listen: it is so hot; I am beginning to sweat. Can you feel the heat? Can you feel it? It is coming from inside! Feel my hand."

She rubbed my hand in hers until my hand felt warm. We stopped running but kept walking fast. I had to work hard to keep up.

"Let's concentrate on the heat inside us. I am beginning to perspire," said my mother.

I started to feel warmer. I was not hot as my mother claimed but I did not feel as cold as before.

She took my hand in hers saying, "It is so hot, look at the steam coming out with my breath. Oh, let's get home so that I can take all this clothing off. Hot, hot, hot. Catch my breath if you can."

She laughed, holding me with one hand and attempting to catch the white steam of her breath with the other. "Hot, hot,

hot," she kept saying as we walked faster and faster toward the house.

"Do you feel the warmth?" asked my mother.

Focused on my mother's words, I relaxed and stopped shaking. By the time we reached the gate of our house, I actually felt warm.

When we got inside, Mum poured some hot chamomile tea into my cup and added extra honey.

"How did you do it?" I asked my mother. "How did you make me stop shivering?"

"It is just mind over matter. You have to believe in whatever you are doing and you will always achieve it."

That advice would guide me on many occasions in the future.

Trnava of my youth

poetry

For my twelfth birthday, which is in October, my mother gave me my first book of poems. Elizabeth Barret Browning's *Sonnets of the Portuguese*. My often-dull world transformed into colors and details I had never noticed before. When the spring came around, I watched the yellow of the daffodils suddenly compete with the color of the early morning sun. When the wind tossed the soft pink petals of the cherry trees in the air, I extended my hands hoping to catch the premise of love in their fragrant softness.

Wrapped in the wake of the spring was my favorite holiday, Easter. I looked forward to the cookies and cakes my mother would make. We would decorate the late-blooming trees with colorful ribbons, and I hoped it would not rain. In our modest garden patch, we had tulips of many colors and two lilac bushes. I arranged the flowers into a vase and brought them into our living room.

"Very nice," said my mother, who was kneading dough for the special Easter cookies she would later let me help her decorate.

"Flowers belong to the garden. They last longer there," observed my father, who did not lift his eyes from the jacket he was sewing.

"Dad took on too much work and everyone wants it for Easter," explained my mother.

I smiled and kissed my dad on his cheek. He was not usually grouchy, but he did have strong and sometimes surprisingly different opinions on seemingly innocuous subjects. Like keeping the flowers in the garden.

In Communist Czechoslovakia, Easter Sunday was a somber affair. Despite the common knowledge of Communist spies lurking in churches and reporting who attended the church's Easter celebration, most people did attend. Both men and women wanted something new to wear, making my father very busy.

Easter Monday, however, was an altogether different affair. As a child I often hid under the bed, from where I would be dragged out and dunked into an ice-cold bathtub by my brothers or taken out and drenched in equally ice-cold buckets of water by friends of my brothers. For this, the boys were rewarded with a splatter of cologne and delectable cookies and cakes my mother would be making the entire week before. The very young boys would get a small coin worth about ten cents.

The tradition was meant to make the girls healthy and strong. This dated back to the days when people lived in villages and the girls were chased for some time before they were caught. Withstanding the cold water was supposed to make them ready for cold winters, something the male population was eager to believe. The girls were also gently whipped by beautifully decorated whips braided from the thin branches of a willow. According to the tale, a willow tree had magical power and by whipping the girl with it, the power of the willow would be transported onto the girl. The number of boys who would visit the girl's house would give her bragging rights through the rest of the year.

The girls in my class talked about boys and a lot of them already wore a bra. I was still skinny and after my October birthday there was not even the slightest sign that things may be changing. By spring, I was the only girl in our class who did not need a bra, and the only "boy" crush I had was on a pop singer. I read and reread the *Sonnets of the Portuguese* hoping to transfer some of the magic on to me. I was definitely ready to love, but I had no real candidate for my affection.

Thanks to my father, who taught me to sew and who always had extra material around, I made myself a bra. Just a simple band with straps, not dissimilar to today's sports bra. My mother's nylon stockings served as fillers. To my untrained eye, it looked remarkably natural. I did not wear the "bra" to school, of course. I wore it while cleaning the house. I figured since I was doing an adult's work, I should look like an adult. I knew my brothers would not be around on cleaning day, lest they should be asked to help. In my "adult" status, I was pleased to do my chores without help.

Baking, however, I did sans my fake chest. It was a special time when I had my mother all to myself. My mother was tall and always wore high heels, even while baking. She would say that wearing flat shoes made her feel as if she were falling over backwards. She had the most exquisite skin despite having never, ever used a single cream. She was not slim but she was not fat, at least not in my eyes. Her smile would disarm an army and her chocolate brown eyes smiled with her but could be equally frightening if you were in trouble. Her hair was her weakness. It was fine and could not make up its mind if it was going to be straight or curly. She called it "weak." Every month she would mix two raw eggs and leave them in her hair for twenty minutes in a hope to make her hair "stronger."

I would like to say that watching my mother bake made me a great baker, but the truth is the time I spent watching her bake had about as much influence on my baking skills as the eggs had on my mother's hair. But, baking for Easter was always special.

Having discovered love, at least on paper, I was looking forward to Easter. I watched my mother working the dough, her apron bulging with her ample bosom, giving me hope that eventually I would take after her. The sun was streaming through the window, lighting her perfect complexion, which, at the risk of sounding conceited, I inherited. I also inherited her dark brown eyes and her height. My hair sits somewhere between my father's, whose vanity was his hair, and my mother's "weak" hair. Both my parents had a wide smile, so I had no way of going wrong there. But to my big disappointment, I would not inherit my mother's generous bosom, and the stocking experience would be useful in future more times than I care to admit.

My mother's hair was covered with a scarf to prevent any hair accidently ending up in the dough. She was up to her elbows, literally, with baking, and Dad was busy finishing several garments he promised to have done by Easter, giving me time to daydream about the upcoming Easter Monday and the boys who would come to our house.

I wished there would be at least one boy who would notice me for me, not as my brothers' little sister. Every so often my mother would ask me to hold on to something or open the oven door. She had a warm smile on her face, as if she knew what I was dreaming about.

Mrs. Balazovicova came in, which was not unusual. She was a seamstress and often came in to ask my father's advice. She was also the only one in the neighborhood who had a telephone. She told my mother my brother Pavel, who was at the soccer practice, was taken to the hospital. The coach called and asked her to let my parents know.

"What did he break this time?" asked Mum with resignation while she was taking off her apron.

"I don't know," said Mrs. Balazovicova. "The coach just said you should come to the hospital right away." My mother's head shot up in alarm.

"What happened?"

"I don't know, you are probably right, playing soccer, what else could it be? The coach and the teacher were there, so I am sure they took care of him, but they want you to pick him up and bring him home."

My mother relaxed. After all, it was not the first time my brother broke a bone. But I noticed that the neighbor did not look at my mother when she was talking.

"You have to carry on with the baking till I get back," said Mother and proceeded to give me instructions. I knew most of it already, but she ran through it with me again, leaving her special recipe notebook open on the counter.

Our neighbor came back shortly after my mother left and spoke to my father, who was sitting at his sewing machine. I could see my father shaking his head. I realized my mother would not be at the hospital yet, so the neighbor knew earlier, when she spoke to my mother, whatever she was telling my father now. What could she be protecting her from?

I almost burned the cookies I had in the oven watching the

animated conversation that I could not hear. I focused on the job at hand and for a while I forgot about the neighbor. I barely managed to keep up with the baking. I did not realize how many different cookies Mother baked and how much work it all was.

The sun was long gone when my father came to ask how I was doing. The light in the kitchen was inadequate; we needed to keep the stronger lights for Dad and his sewing and we had only so many high-voltage lightbulbs.

"Pavel had his appendix out," said Dad. "He will be fine, but Mum is going to stay with him...So, can you finish the baking? I have someone coming to pick up a jacket in about an hour, then I would like to go to the hospital too."

"Where is Jan?" I asked.

"Reading," said Dad.

"Don't worry, he will not starve with all this food around." I knew he would feast on all the cookies.

"Good, so I am going to finish the jacket."

I nodded and felt very important. I went to my secret drawer and put on my bra. If ever there was a reason to look the part I was unexpectedly expected to play, this was it! I stuffed in an extra stocking. I knew my father was too busy to notice and I had some woman's work to do, so I deserved the extra help.

Time flew by. I heard the doorbell.

"Can you get it? I am finishing with the jacket. You know where to take him." I heard my father call out to me.

I was familiar with the routine.

Our house had three big rooms and one small room we called our "summer" kitchen. We used it only for baking. Usually for Easter, Christmas, and for special celebration. The third room was always neat and clean in case we got unexpected visitors and for my father's customers to try on their clothes. The room also had a big mirror with three parts so that if you turned the adjustable sides just right, you could see your own back. This was mainly used for Dad's clients.

I opened the door and almost fainted. Right there in front of me stood the most beautiful young boy I had ever seen. His name was Andrej, and finally I had someone to be in love with.

He was taller than me, had shining blue eyes, blond, tight-curly hair, and a smile that could have melted the entire North Pole.

I walked him to the room with the mirror and switched on the light. I caught sight of a stranger with my mother's scarf covering her hair, a red skirt that was meant to be worn on special occasions, and a white fitted shirt my dad made me despite my mother's protests. My eyes were shining, and my smile went practically around my head. Bulging from my shirt were my fake boobs.

My dad walked in with the jacket, but I stood rooted to the floor. Nether Andrej nor my father noticed I was still there. I smelled the cookies and ran to the kitchen.

Before Andrej left, he poked his head into the kitchen and said, "Something smells good."

My father wrapped a couple of cookies for him, and he smiled at me a smile that would give the *Sonnets of the Portuguese* whole new meaning. I would live on it through the whole summer.

My brother Pavel came home the next day and recovered enough to go with our brother Jan on the usual Easter rounds.

a song for kristina

Every month, on her payday, my mother bought one vinyl record of her choosing. It was a gift to herself in lieu of the flowers my father had never bought for her. An exchange the whole family benefited from.

Sometime during my sixth year, my mother came home with a record she said she bought for my father. Our record player was in the room where he sewed and as usual, he was busy.

"Put it on," said Dad. "I can listen while I work."

I sat at the table with my mother and for the first time I heard *A Song for Kristina*. My father did not look up from his work but at the end of the song, he blew his nose loudly.

The song's description of the young woman was so eloquent that, as I listened, I could see a familiar photograph and the young woman in it came alive.

In my childhood bedroom, we had four beds shared by my parents and three children. My brothers, who were older than I, each had their own bed. I was the wanderer who slept on any space that was available. Once I reached age five, my brothers refused to let me in their beds because, apparently, I kicked while sleeping. So mostly, I slept between my parents. My father often worked nights and so I would sleep on his side of the bed. When I looked up, I would see the smiling portrait of my father's first wife, Kristina.

My mother told me even before I could fully understand it, that my father loved his first wife very much, but one terrible morning, after he woke up, he went to kiss her good morning, and she was cold. She had died during the night. I learned later that she had died of an aneurysm. The song brought to life a woman I would never know but I would always remember.

The original Kristina

* * *

My mother worked at the railway station and she was offered a promotion that hinged on three conditions: she take a specific secretarial course, commute to a nearby village, half an hour on the bus each way, and take a first aid course. The village was not far from Trnava where we lived, but too far if anyone needed urgent medical help, hence the need to put someone in the village who could administer first aid. For my education-hungry mother, two of the conditions were a dream come true and she was willing to accept the third, the travel, to get the other two. The promotion and more money were quite secondary to her.

One year into her job, she was called to a house in the village, where a young woman had passed out. Her neighbor who called, reported to my mother, "We were talking and suddenly she said she felt dizzy and lay down on the floor. I thought I would wait with her till she felt better but I have been here an hour and she does not look better."

After checking the woman's pulse, all my mother could do was to call an ambulance from Trnava with the doctor, who confirmed my mother's analysis; the woman was dead.

My mother was quite shaken when she learned that, incredibly, the deceased woman's name was Kristina and the doctor's report confirmed she had died of an aneurysm.

This Kristina had a one-year-old daughter who was asleep while the neighbor waited for her mother to feel better. Once the grim circumstance had been confirmed, the child had to be taken care of. A relative was called to come and take care of the little girl.

Kristina's husband, Lorenzo, was devastated and quite unable to take care of anything. With the baby girl being taken care of by her aunt, my mother turned to the funeral arrangements. Then, she called Lorenzo's work. She explained the situation and got him some extra time off.

My mother brought Lorenzo to our house and together with my father, who was amazed by the pair of coincidences and understood only too well Lorenzo's pain and the feeling of loss, they helped him through the early days. Eventually Lorenzo was able to go back to work.

Lorenzo ran a wine tavern in Trnava. He was taller than my father, but had far less hair and his was lighter. He was also much fatter than my father, who was very slim. My father had a warm, wide smile; Lorenzo laughed loudly, which I did not like. The tavern closed at nine p.m., and Lorenzo would stop at our house before he rode his motorbike back to his village. I often waited with my mother on the nights he was stopping by and I remember I did not like it.

Any time the tavern was closed, Lorenzo was at our house. He talked about his daughter, Mary, a lot, how well she was doing with her aunt, but he seemed in no hurry to be with her.

Eventually, Lorenzo announced that he was bringing Mary to meet me. Despite our age difference—she was six years younger—I was looking forward to have a girl to play with. I was tired of my brothers pushing me around. Lorenzo dropped Mary off at our house on his way to work. By then, she was three years old.

"I will be back soon," said Lorenzo. My mother and I stood in our kitchen, each holding one of Mary's hands.

"You be a good girl." Lorenzo bent down to kiss his daughter on the forehead, then he left.

"Would you like to take Mary out into the yard and play with her?" asked my mother.

The day smelled of spring and the weather was comfortably warm. Eagerly I agreed. Finally, I had a girl to play with, even if she were younger than me.

Holding Mary's hand, I walked her out to our yard. She was a thin little girl with hauntingly dark eyes, straight brown hair, and a slightly lopsided smile. We played for a little while with my old pram that my mum brought down from the attic, including my American doll and the collection of dresses that Dad and I made for the doll. I let Mary dress the doll, which she seemed to enjoy.

I don't know how long we played, when without warning Mary began to cry for no apparent reason, at least not to me. She dropped the doll on the ground; I was not sure if accidentally or on purpose. I tried to comfort her but soon realized I was in over my head and called my mother. But my mother was no more successful than I was. Mary's crying was not angry or sad, just relentless.

It would be a long time before Mary came to our house again. The same could not be said about Lorenzo. He thanked me endlessly for playing with Mary and he hugged me and kissed me, something I disliked.

At that time my mother had asked to be transferred back to Trnava. The commute had begun to be too much for her. The family welcomed the change. But I did not like that Lorenzo was spending more and more time at our house, even coming for dinner, although he was always very respectful and friendly toward my father.

One evening in spring Lorenzo suggested an outing the following Sunday. My mother could go with him on his motorbike, Lorenzo suggested, and I could go with my father because he owned a much less powerful motorbike.

The next several months became a friendship I never understood. Except perhaps blind empathy.

We would go to visit my mother's village, my father's village, farms where we bought apples, pears, and potatoes for the winter. In fall we went to fairs until the cold weather stopped the biking excursions. Often, we would lose sight of Lorenzo's motorbike and find him and my mother already at the appointed destination.

During the school winter holiday, my mother, who had a big discount on trains because she worked for the railway, took my brothers to the High Tatra mountains. Lorenzo went with them. My father was too busy to go just before Christmas and I faked an illness. Grandmother Katarina knew I was not sick but helped me to stay behind.

After that, a house on our street came up for sale. Lorenzo bought it and moved in. Mary became a fixture in our house. The first euphoria of having a sister disappeared quickly. Mary, by this time six years old, became difficult. She was prone to outbursts of tears or laughter that lasted for hours, often mixed together.

Lorenzo said he was thankful for the time I spent playing with Mary, but he thanked me too often and hugged me too much. He called my mother Mary's new mummy. Grandmother Katarina did not like it and insisted that Lorenzo hire full-time childcare.

In spring, my mother volunteered to be a chaperone for my brother's class trip to Prague. Once again, Lorenzo went with her.

Soon after they got back, I overheard my mother saying to my father, "You believe an anonymous letter?" I had never heard the word *anonymous* before, but instinctively I knew what it implied. The atmosphere in our house had become one of deafening silence. I blamed Lorenzo. I began to hate him.

The situation had become tense and very upsetting to me. The following week, my brothers and I went to a swim meet for a weekend. Pointedly I said "goodbye" from a distance to my parents but I came back to hug grandmother Katarina.

When my brothers and I got back from the swim meet, my parents were talking. More than talking. They were laughing and Mum even kissed Dad on his cheek. Grandmother Katarina had fish for dinner, which she loved and my mother approved of. Definitely a meeting of minds had taken place. Whatever the problem, it was no more. For a brief time, I was happy.

Six months later, my grandmother Katarina died. Lorenzo came to express his condolences. Often. He said he wanted to repay my mother's kindness in his time of need. Soon, he came every day. With Grandmother Katarina gone, I noticed he never missed an opportunity to hug me and kiss me. He wanted me to sit on his lap. I was ten years old and way past sitting on anybody's lap. He kissed me all over my face, which I loathed and washed my face as soon as I could. Then he started to stick his tongue in my mouth, and I began to hate him even more than I already did.

I confided to my brother Jan about the tongue and he told me Lorenzo did that to him too. My brother's words made me feel a little better. Perhaps Lorenzo really was just affectionate and lonely. So, I tried to ignore it as much as I could.

I also avoided him as much as I could. But I was not a good actress. I was cold and he was probably not wrong when he complained to my mother that I was rude. Instinctively I knew not to say anything to my father. I noticed my father had less time for Lorenzo. When there was a free Sunday, our family went out together without Lorenzo.

The summer arrived and I was able to put Lorenzo out of my mind. I was happy to spend my time hanging out at the swimming pool. I never felt lonely when I was among people. I did not need someone to talk to. My imagination was enough to keep me company. I would smile happily while getting an even suntan.

Then, the day of our last swim practice at the outdoor pool, I felt weak and cold. I got out to go to the bathroom. The coach stopped me before I got back into the water.

"You don't look right. Here is a towel; dry yourself off and sit next to me for a while." A few minutes later I felt warm enough to get back in, but the coach touched my forehead and told me to get dressed and go home.

The walk home was at least half a kilometer. By the time I got to our gate, I could barely move. I had no key because I was supposed to go home with my brothers, who were still at the pool. I rang the bell. I knew my father was away in Bratislava visiting his sick brother. He would not be home till the next day. But my mother was supposed to be home. She would come soon to the gate and take care of me. I was sure.

But nobody came. I could barely move and it required a supreme effort to keep myself standing. I leaned against the cold stone on our gate and slowly slid and sat on the pavement.

I thought I saw blood on the gate.

My whole body ached, and I was periodically hot and cold. I sat there for what seemed to me a very long time. I could see more blood on the pavement but my eyelids hurt when I tried to keep them open so I closed them and the blood disappeared. The neighbor from across the street saw me and brought me to her house and put me in her bed. I knew she had a key to our house and I asked her why she was not taking me home and where my mother was and why there was blood on the gate, but she just shushed me as if I were a baby and did not answer.

My temperature spiked so high, I started to hallucinate. The doctor came. I had a deep sense of fear. I kept asking for my mother but was told to try to sleep.

Two days later I woke up and found myself in my house, in my father's bed. I heard my mother crying and my father looking at me with a deep line in his forehead. The doctor said there was an Asian flu running rampant and several people had died. I did not, but I did miss the first day of school.

* * *

From the time I reached the house with the fever that day, I knew something was amiss. During my recovery I often pretended to be asleep when my mother talked to her best friend and our neighbor. When I learned the facts, they became a weight I would have to carry alone.

While we were all at the pool and my father was in Bratislava, Lorenzo came to our house knowing my mother would be alone. Our house was surrounded by an iron fence, which was as much to keep us kids in as it was to keep intruders out. The gate had spikes at the top, which my brother and I would climb over when we forgot our keys.

Lorenzo came in that early afternoon and proclaimed his never-ending love to my mother. When she categorically refused him, he became aggressive and tried to rape her. She ran out and tried to climb over the gate. She must have slipped and a spike pierced her upper thigh. Lorenzo got frightened and helped her down, then, unlocking the gate, he ran to the neighbor across the street, the only one with a telephone, to call an ambulance. How my mother explained her injury to my father I will never know. She required stiches but the wound was not too deep and she was able to come home the same day.

* * *

Lorenzo still came to the house. My mother had to keep the attack a secret to protect her family. As a child, I kept my knowledge for the sake of my father. Later, as a woman, I recognized the agony my mother had to go through. To save her at least some of the pain, I never told her I knew.

My mother still continued to help with Mary. I kept away from Lorenzo but I was not afraid of him anymore. Knowing what he was capable of gave me a sense of preparedness. When I heard that he was diagnosed with cancer, I felt relieved.

In the next two years he was in and out of the hospital. Despite everything, my mother felt sorry for Lorenzo. I did not mind bringing him soup or a kolache my mother would make. I would always sit out of reach despite the invitations to hold his hand. Eventually he stopped asking. Not because he did not want me to hold his hand but because he no longer had the strength to ask.

I was at the railway station with my swim team, leaving for a meet, when I learned that Lorenzo had died. I could not control my emotion, nor could I control my facial expression. I smiled.

For years I felt guilty about that. The memory of it was frighteningly clear. Imagine being glad that someone died. I knew life dealt him a raw deal, but I could not help comparing him to my father, who did not *use* others to heal his own wound when *his* Kristina died.

I no longer feel guilty. I know now I was relieved that I, and my whole family, would be free of a person who would use anyone to fill his emptiness regardless of the costs to the other people.

I had often struggled with the question, how deep was my father's sympathy? After Lorenzo died and after nobody from her family wanted to take care of Mary, I found out the answer. The state took over her welfare, put her up for adoption, and my parents adopted Mary. For a while I thought that had answered the depth of my father's sympathy. But I was wrong. It was not sympathy for Lorenzo. The reason my father agreed to take on Mary was he loved children. It was as simple as that.

We had never learned anything about Mary's mother or her family. In the past, every so often Lorenzo had mentioned some aunt who lived in England and when she came back, instead of saying yes, she would always say, all right. That, literally, was all we knew of Mary's family.

In some way it was easier for her to become part of our family. She was treated the same as the three of us and she was loved equally. My father had endless patience with her, which influenced me deeply. I tried to exercise the same patience, which for a teenager was not always easy.

We all knew on some level that Mary did not belong in a regular school. But at that time, children who had special needs, once labeled as such, were almost always destined to spend their life in an institution. My mother wanted to spare Mary from that fate. My mother pushed and pulled, using friendships and sympathy to get her through the eight years of mandatory education.

Mary grew up tall and slim, with a pale complexion that set off her dark eyes. She was pretty with a slightly lopsided smile.

Her hair lightened some from her childhood days but remained very straight. She often had a faraway look that made her seem intriguing to strangers. Once Mary finished her education, my mother secured her a job in a local snack bar. She knew the manager and he owed her a favor. To protect Mary from unkind people, her official title was the manager's assistant, but essentially, she did the job of a busboy.

* * *

During the entire time that Mary lived with us, the government paid my mother every month a sum of money that was quite generous. My mother put the money into a savings account. When Mary turned eighteen, the money stopped and my mother bought her an apartment, which she rented out and continued to put the money into Mary's saving account.

By then, I was in England and my mother was battling cancer. With me gone and my brothers about to get married, my mother did not want to leave the responsibility of Mary to my father. With the apartment, she secured Mary's financial independence and in future a place to live. For the time being, however, Mary continued to live with my parents.

Once Mary learned that she owned an apartment, she became discontented. She did not want to be watched over by my parents anymore. The situation became complicated. We all knew on some level that Mary should not live alone. But empowered by the knowledge that she owned an apartment, she became very difficult, even aggressive. She pressed my mother to let her live in her apartment on a trial basis. She could be very persuasive and determined. In the end, my mother reasoned, it was better if Mary tried to live alone while she could still watch over her.

The apartment was rented furnished so all that was needed was to give it a good cleaning for Mary to move in. My father made Mary new curtains for the apartment, and she moved in. For a year or two, all was well. But then, Mary became sexually active. She changed the locks on her apartment so my parents could not check in on her. If she had a boyfriend, that would have been fine, but she literally chased young boys for sex. The young men serving their mandatory two-year military service were the ones who usually obliged. This, we learned later from the police because she removed my mother as a next of kin, which hurt my mother deeply.

One day Mary did not turn up for work. The first day was not very unusual, but the second was. Mary never missed two days as she did not cook and existed exclusively on the food she got in the snack bar. It was part of her pay.

On the third morning her boss called the police, who broke into Mary's apartment. They found her naked and unconscious, locked in the closet. She was taken to the hospital, where, after mental evaluation, doctors concluded that she had to be moved into a mental institution.

My mother was sad, but she also knew she could not protect Mary anymore. She sold Mary's apartment and put the money into the bank so Mary could treat herself to chocolate. She loved chocolate. She was allowed supervised outings as well, so the money would let her afford that too.

My brothers went to visit when they could. Mary was also allowed to come to my father's funeral and she also received permission to stay with my mother for a few days. But she went to town straight from the cemetery and she was up to her old tricks.

She was taken back to the institution. Not long after, Mary died in her sleep. The cause of death: liver failure. She was thirty years old.

After Mary's death, I struggled with the legacy of *A Song for Kristina*. The song no longer represented only the smiling woman above my head every time I woke up on my father's side of the bed. The song reminded me of the other Kristina, whose legacy was Mary. As hard as it was for me to admit it, there was a link between Mary's indiscriminate appetite for sex and Lorenzo's misjudgment of propriety. I began to wonder whether Lorenzo was truly a predator, or had he suffered with hormonal and mental imbalance like Mary.

A Song for Kristina still steers powerful emotions inside me. But I no longer blame myself for the happiness I felt at the news of Lorenzo's death, and I am able to cry for him.

apple cider

The Cold War was as cold as ever when my brothers and I grew up behind the Iron Curtain in Communist Czechoslovakia. Autumn was the time to store food that we planned to eat in the winter. We had no refrigerator, but we did have a big, cold cellar. My father made all the shelves in the cellar, and I liked to help.

"Hold the wood while I cut it," said Dad with authority. I loved to watch the white sawdust fall on my shoes. I pretended that it was powdered sugar and my shoes were the kolach that my mother would eventually make. I pictured the big, juicy apples, pears, and plums that would sit and wait on this very shelf until it was time to use them. We put the vegetables in the darkest and coolest part of the cellar while the fruit was kept on the lighter side. It was essential that our provisions last until the first rays of the spring sun allowed farmers to plant the new crop.

Every year I rubbed mineral oil into the wood of the shelves until they were as smooth as the plush velvet gloves my mother would wear on special occasions. The smell of the oil seemed to enhance the delicate aroma of each fruit. I could feel the moisture swell in my mouth at the thought of biting into one of the fragrant jewels proudly decorating the walls of the cellar. The hues of green, red, and purple looked like the mosaic necklace that sparkled around my mother's neck.

Ah, my mother! She would turn those riches into the most delectable dishes. When she cooked, the intoxicating aroma would wake us kids up as it traveled to our bedroom. We followed the scent, which inevitably led us to the old wood-fired stove covered by heavy pots full of bubbling dishes. A bouquet of tarragon, sage, and thyme enhanced by slivers of garlic would linger in midair like a prelude to a symphony. The memory of feasting on those rainbow-colored vegetables still reduces me to a drooling child.

To divide the vegetables and fruits, Dad decided to separate the two sections of the cellar. Since he was a tailor, we always had extra fabric. To protect the delicate aroma of the fruit from the vegetables' robust smell, Dad and I sewed a patchwork curtain that reflected the personality of both rooms.

We started with soft, delicate cotton that smelled as pure as the air after the rain. The colors of the fabrics intensified as if to match the pale green plums that the heat of summer would turn deep orange, blue, and purple. I stroked the fine wool patches, colors of which reminded me of carrots, rutabaga, and potatoes.

For the second half of the curtain, fabrics became heavier in order to weigh the curtain down. For the bottom, Dad found a piece of dark leather reminiscent of the richness of the earth that nourished the splendor waiting on the shelves to be enjoyed in the long winter months.

Even at the end of the winter, as our stores ran out, my mother managed to perform her magic. The carrots lightly sweetened the soup, while parsnips added a hint of tartness. To add substance, she sliced deep green kale leaves that reminded us of the soccer fields of summer. But the highlight was always the crisp flesh of the dark purple kohlrabi. It required Mum's touch to cook everything just right so that none of the flavors escaped.

Even more than preparing the cellar, however, apple cider heralded the arrival of autumn. The spicy aroma of nutmeg, cinnamon, cloves, and dark sugar was an unmistakable calling card for the delights to be enjoyed in days to come. The Grand Central of our family was a big room in which the honored space was allocated to the wooden barrel containing the apple cider.

One year the apples were so plentiful, my parents bought double the usual amount, confident that their three growing,

always-on-the-move children would have no problem consuming them. Even when the weather turned cold, we still had plenty of cider. Suddenly, late in the autumn, we were blessed with an Indian summer. My brothers and I played soccer all afternoon and, when darkness forced us inside, we were parched. Thirstily we drank the cider from the wooden barrel.

As most siblings do, we used to argue about nonsense. But on this occasion, my grandmother, who lived with us, was thrilled to see all three of us taking turns playing checkers with my father's shirt buttons from the big chest he kept on his sewing machine table. So she was delighted to give her daughter an excellent report: "No bickering, the children were a delight."

Perhaps a little *too* delightful. My mother watched us laughing for the pure joy of laughing. Suspicious, she came closer to her giggling children. She took a sip from the fermented cider and, realizing the source of our mirth, said in horror, "Mama, they are drunk!"

grandmother katarina

Grandmother Katarina, my mother's mother, was seventy-eight years old when she died. Her face, resting on a black lace pillow in the casket, will be etched into my memory forever. To me she looked peaceful and very beautiful.

Katarina came to live with us before I was born. She stayed for twelve years, most of which she was confined to bed. She was a tall, big-boned woman with high cheekbones and dark brown eyes.

I have only a single memory of her walking.

It was a beautiful spring day and she asked me to help her put on her shoes. She wore a richly gathered black cotton skirt that fell just short of her ankles. I could not believe how big her feet were. Her shoes seemed to be walking ahead of her. I later thought that her courage matched her feet.

Having been left alone, abandoned with her five children, she was not afraid to break the rules of her era. Small rebellions by today's standards, but brave during her time. She did not attend church because Katarina believed God would hear her no matter where she was. When her husband left her and went to France, she ignored the stigma and called herself a widow. In her mind he was dead and that was what mattered to her. Yet, when her son Juraj wanted to go to France to see his father, she let him go, even helped with the money for the journey, unafraid of the new gossip it would bring.

There was a certain mystery about Grandmother Katarina that nobody in the family ever spoke of loud enough for a child like me

My mother is the one with short hair. The other young lady
is my aunt Katarina who was an unpublished writer.

to hear or understand. But she liked to stir the pot of imagination of a child and I was an eager recipient.

One day she told me that if she were born a hundred years earlier, she would have been burned at the stake. Seeing the fear in my eyes, she added with a mischievous smile, "But, there would have been a huge storm with an enormous amount of rain that would have put out the fire; the empty heads would have thought that I had special power and would have feared me!" She loved that image. She patted me on my head and said, "Don't fear stupid people."

* * *

My father was considered a parasite by the Communist government of Czechoslovakia, because he had formerly owned a tailor shop with seven employees. The best job he could find was as a night watchman in a local factory. The job, however, had a positive side to it. It meant that my father was home to see us off to school while my mother, being born more suitably poor, had a day job at the local railway station as a secretary. I now think of him as a pioneer stay-at-home dad. It was also comforting for my mother to know that Grandmother Katarina was not at home alone.

On cold winter mornings when Dad would just get home from work, he would let us kids dash from the bedroom into my grandmother's bed, which would be heavenly warm. We knew that Mum, who was a stickler for manners, would be horrified to see us all in Grandmother's bed having breakfast, but she was not there and we would not tell. And Grandmother, who loved her grandchildren and a good bit of mischief, loved it too.

The night job also allowed my father to have a thriving tailoring business during the day. Unofficial, of course. He did not need much sleep. He would sleep for ten minutes and be refreshed. He called those naps, "Napoleons." Avid reader of history he would tell me that Napoleon slept only 10 minutes at the time. My father took the opportunity while his irons were warming up on the kitchen's big stove. Grandma would help by removing support stitches from the garments once they were no longer needed.

While working, the two enjoyed talking about many subjects, not skirting the controversial ones. My father was spiritual but a firm atheist. Katarina was devoted to God, but with her own set of rules. She prayed sitting on her bed with her head bowed; she moved her lips without sound. Her prayers were always between her and her God. At a time when the Communists kept their spies in churches, Katarina often told me, "God listens to us no matter where we are."

My father and Katarina did agree on one major subject: They both blamed the Communists AND religion for the problems troubling the world.

* * *

The living room was the hub of our family life. We cooked and ate there, we did our homework there, Dad made all his garments in there, and Grandmother Katarina lived and slept there. The bedroom was where the rest of us slept.

On the coldest nights in the winter, my father would light the fire in the bedroom's small coal stove. He let it burn just long enough to take the chill out of the air for me and my two brothers to make it under the warm goose down.

One very cold and unusually long winter we were running out of coal and could not waste it on frivolities like warming up the bedroom. My father watched his children gathering their courage to brave the frigid room, when he got an idea. He selected a couple of his irons, which were always on the stove in the kitchen ready for his use. Picking the two he deemed cool enough, he wrapped them in old towels and put them at the bottom of the bed. We were excited at the prospect of any part of our body getting some warmth.

When Dad decided it was the right time, we ran into the bedroom and jockeyed for the best position for our feet. Suddenly, despite the sound of our chattering teeth, we heard a tearing sound, then my feet felt something soft and warm. None of us said anything, but reflexively we pulled our legs up to our chins.

"Is your father a genius?" asked Dad when he came to pick up his irons. He was visibly disappointed by the silence he received.

"Good night," he said tersely. As he lifted the duvet to get his irons, soft white particles ascended toward the ceiling. Soon our father's black hair was decorated with white feathers and his bewildered expression made it clear that he had no idea about the source of the white avalanche. We forgot about the cold and jumped from behind the covers onto the bed and shrieked with delight, trying to catch the flying feathers.

The pandemonium had to be explained to Grandmother Katarina, who appreciated the humor of it and seldom missed an opportunity to tell visitors how her son-in-law could make it snow indoors.

* * *

Katarina was unable to exercise but loved to eat rich food, so the doctor put her on a strict diet. But when she checked the list of foods approved by her doctor, she looked at him with sincerity and said: "If this is all that I can eat, I can die tomorrow."

"Lean meat?" said Katarina with the doctor barely out of earshot.

"How could pork be lean?" she scoffed. "Has the doctor ever seen a pig? And no salt? Then why did God make the oceans salty?" She looked at my mother, challenging her to reply.

Katarina's motto became, "Give me love and good food while I am alive instead of flowers on my grave."

Dad was an unwitting enabler. Anytime he found something Katarina liked, he would come in and, with great ceremony, declare that he had brought her a wreath for her grave. With the excitement of a child, she would unwrap the item to see what goody she had received. Sometimes it would be the first strawberries of the season, which my mother would approve of. But sometimes it would be goose liver, which would put a deep frown on my mother's forehead. Dad would look sheepishly at her and declare, "Once in a while, there has to be a party, even in Hell," which sounds much more logical in Slovak.

Katarina had a good run ignoring the doctor's advice. But in the end, she paid for her defiance.

I was first to come home from school that day and found my father sitting by my grandmother's bed. Before I took my coat off, Dad sent me to fetch my mother from work. I ran most of the way and delivered the message. She put me on the back of her bicycle and pedaled home as fast as she could.

When we arrived, Grandmother Katarina was sitting in the bed and her eyes were closed. My father left to get the doctor. My brothers were home from school by then and Mother told us to go out and play. One of our neighbors came over, gave us dinner, then told us to go to the bedroom and read.

I snuck into the living room and crouched in the corner opposite the bed where my grandmother lay in my mother's arms. Her breathing was raspy. My mother stroked her forehead the way she used to stroke mine when I was sick.

Suddenly my grandmother's body stretched violently in my mother's arms as if to get a deep breath. I waited for her to breathe out, but she did not. She fell against my mother's chest, and I knew I had witnessed death.

My mother kissed Grandmother Katarina on the forehead and laid her gently in the bed. I pressed my spine into the wall when the door into the room opened, and I saw the silhouette of my Grandmother Katarina standing in the doorway. For a brief moment her face became clear, and she looked directly into my eyes, and I heard her say, "Don't fear stupid people." Then the silhouette dissolved into darkness and my eyes filled with tears, but I was not afraid.

thieves

As the first winter without my grandmother approached, my brothers, eleven and ten, were deemed old enough to be left alone in the house with me, while our parents were still at work. As the daylight got rapidly shorter, I was not sure if it was the darkness outside of the windows or the unknown that scared me. But there was strength in numbers and there were three of us.

We had no TV, so we each found something to do. My brother Jan was reading Jules Verne's *Twenty Thousand Leagues under the Sea*, brother Pavel was engrossed in *The Hound of the Baskervilles,* and I was listening to a play on the radio called *Yasnaya Polyana*, a play popular with the Communist government as it told the story how Tolstoy rejected fame and money and preferred peasants to aristocracy.

I preferred radio to reading, not just because the story would come alive in dialog but also because it allowed my hands to do something else. In that instance, with winter on the horizon, I was knitting a scarf.

The heat in the room came from the large stove that had to be fed with coal. We took turns going out and getting more coal from the shed located in our yard where we kept our supplies.

The play had finished, and I switched the radio off. For a while there was silence, interrupted only by the tick-tock of the clock on the wall, and the soft sound of my knitting needles as they rubbed against each other at regular intervals.

Suddenly, we heard a sound coming from the coal shed. We all looked up and froze.

"Did you hear that?" asked Pavel.

Jan walked over to the window and put his face right against it. He used his hands to block the light from the room so that he could see outside. I put down my knitting needles.

"The door to the coal shed is open and I can see two men stealing our coal," reported my brother.

"What shall we do?" My voice quivered.

"We have to kill them," said Pavel.

Clearly his mind was under the influence of the book he was reading.

"You are crazy." Jan dismissed the idea.

Pavel had a flair for dramatics. Being eldest, Jan took charge.

"I will take the biggest knife we have. Pavel, you take Dad's scissors and you..." Jan pointed at me. "...you take your knitting needles."

I gasped, looking at my brothers armed with knife and scissors. My father was a tailor and his scissors were not an ordinary size. They were very big and heavy.

"First we challenge them to leave the coal and go away," Jan said, but I could see Pavel being skeptical. He wanted more action.

Jan switched off the light in the room, so that the thieves would not see us leaving. After a short pause he led us out of the dark room, with Pavel and me close behind him.

Meanwhile, the thieves went about their business. By the time we inched outside into the yard, despite the dark, starless sky, my eyes had adapted, and I started to see a little. It looked to me as if the thieves were organizing the shed, rather than stealing the coal, but I kept quiet. As we inched closer, Jan was still leading but Pavel pushed me ahead of him.

"I'll protect your back," he whispered.

Our yard was not very big, so it did not take us long to get close to the thieves.

"Drop the bucket and run!" shouted Jan, as he raised his hand that held the knife, and with his free hand he pushed me in front of him like a shield. I was trembling while Jan squeezed my shoulder. I started to cry. One of the thieves trained his flashlight at us, blinding us.

"You are a fine hero, pushing your little sister in front of you," said our father. His friend, who indeed was helping him to organize the shed, burst out laughing.

My brothers never lived down what became family folklore that they had hidden behind their little sister.

uncle pavel

According to the local records in Czechoslovakia, my grandparents had three boys named Pavel, two of whom died in early infancy. My grandfather's name was not Pavel, which begged the question why having a son with that name was so important to them.

To my disappointment, there was no mystery. Once they decided on a name, my grandparents saw no reason to look for another name until that one was taken. And so, at last my Uncle Pavel was born and thrived.

Of all his siblings, my father was closest to his brother Pavel. My father and I often visited Pavel and his wife, Anna. They lived in the mountains above Myjava, the town where my father was born. The distance was within the capability of the small motorbike my father owned, so I would hop on the back seat and off we went.

Uncle Pavel greeted us warmly, holding his inevitable cigarette away from me. He spoke softly and I always thought that his smile was sad. The house was really just one room, which was divided among three areas: living, sleeping, and kitchen. A large stove dominated the corner of the room close to a wooden cabinet that held all the plates, pots, and utensils the cook would need to create fine dishes, including my Aunt Anna's fragrant lavender cookies I was lucky enough to sample.

In her youth, Anna was famed for her beautiful raven hair. But I only knew her with her hair a silvery-white. Hers was one of those stories you did not remember when or how you first heard it, but once you heard it, you would never forget.

* * *

WWII was raging when one winter night two German soldiers on patrol secured a bottle of Slivovica to keep themselves warm, no doubt under the threat of a gun.

Encouraged by the alcohol, the soldiers decided to look for partisans who they thought could be hiding in the house close to the mountain. They found a mother and daughter huddled by the fire. By then, the soldiers were more than just warmed up by the Slivovica and decided to show the Slovak peasants who was in charge, ordering the women to take them to the partisans. They marched the two terrified women out into the yard, where one of the soldiers noticed a shovel.

"Take the shovel," he ordered. My Aunt Anna understood German and followed the order.

The alcohol was a shield against the icy wind, but the two soldiers found it hard to walk, even though the women had cleared the path for them with the shovel. In his drunken haze one of the soldiers decided that the women were leading them into a trap.

"We should just shoot them and go back!" he shouted to his partner over the howling wind. Anna, half frozen, thought a fast death might be preferable. She said nothing to her mother.

"Dig your grave," barked the drunken soldier.

"They want us to dig a hole for the bottle," Anna told her mother. But the pain in her mother's eyes told her that her mother knew what they were doing. It was a mother's pain for the daughter whom she could not save. As they labored on the frozen ground, Anna noticed that the Germans, by now totally drunk, had found a fallen tree and sat down.

It did not take long before they started to snore. Mother and daughter ran back to the village and hid in the house of a friend, but the soldiers never came back for them. Some people said that an officer found the patrolmen with an empty bottle next to them and he shot them. Nobody ever found their bodies, so my aunt never knew for sure what happened, but in the morning her hair was completely white.

* * *

When we arrived at the home of my aunt and uncle, the table would be covered with a white damask tablecloth laden with delicious goodies made from the wild berries and freshly made for our arrival. A large container with chamomile tea already sweetened with honey and freshly squeezed lemon, saved for visitors only, was placed in the middle of the table, with the ladle next to it so that we could help ourselves. There were no teapots in Czechoslovakia.

During the war, Uncle Pavel worked with the Slovak resistance. He was a writer and an editor for an underground paper that helped to keep everybody informed and ahead of the German troops that occupied the country. He spent a lot of time hiding. Smoking helped to pass the time. He told us many stories about the danger people put themselves into, and often paid for with their lives, to help him and his friends.

I like to think that I got my love of writing from my Uncle Pavel.

* * *

The partisans would come down from the mountains dressed in the local costumes so that the Germans would not recognize them. They had arranged with local people to pick up ammunition supplies as well as provisions of food and clothing. For that same reason, the Germans and the Gestapo, who were much worse, kept a close eye on the villagers.

Closest to Pavel's post in the mountains was a small tavern owned by the widow of Milos Kolar, who had died of tuberculosis just before the war. The widow gave the partisans food, often washed their clothing, and whenever she could she, gave them money. She often fed Pavel, even if it meant that she would go without food.

The Germans recruited some Slovaks, who joined the Gestapo. These traitors were used to find out who collaborated with the partisans. Dressed in local clothes, one of the Gestapo Slovaks told the Widow Kolar that he had to warn the partisans about danger coming their way. She gave him food and drink, but at the last minute, she had a bad feeling. She sent him to the part of the mountain where she knew partisans had left months before.

A few hours later, the Gestapo took her away. While she was in prison close to Myjava, her daughter could bring her food every day. Two weeks later, they took her to Senica. Her daughter could visit only once a week. After that, they took her to Dachau. The last time her daughter came to see her mother, she was told by one of the prisoners that like so many others, they tortured her to death.

After the war, Uncle Pavel was haunted by Stalin's minions and barely escaped prison. He found solace in the mountains that once again gave him protection.

The last time I saw my Uncle Pavel was just before I left for England. My father and I visited him at the hospital. He had throat cancer. I remember he had an open hole in his throat the size of a golf ball, which I tried hard not to look at. He hugged me tight and wished me luck. The memory of the cookies on his and Anna's table had overridden the smell of the hospital disinfectant and I told him I could still smell the lavender on him, even dressed as he was in hospital pajamas. He smiled his sad smile.

the leather jacket

My father was barely old enough to remember his sister Dorka when she left for America. She was twenty years old, petite in stature and not rebellious by nature. Before she left, her parents betrothed her to Jan, a neighbor's boy. They grew up together and he would take care of her on the long journey, they reasoned. Betrothing, even marrying their children before they left home, gave the parents a certain amount of peace.

On the boat, Dorka and Jan befriended Dan and Ana, another couple also from Slovakia, also newly betrothed. The two couples were bonded by their heritage, their customs, and their native language. By the time they stepped off the boat, they were in love, but not in the way that was expected.

Dan, a tall, lanky young man with a booming voice, married the petite Dorka, who'd been betrothed to Jan. And Jan married Ana, who was betrothed to Dan. The two couples were brought together by the winds that shifted humanity from place to place and were separated by the same power of chance, never to see each other again.

Back home, my father, who was young enough for his presence to be ignored by the adults when they talked about important things, overheard them talk about Dorka—now Dorothy—and the fact that she'd married some young man she met on the boat instead the fine man they had found for her. "She fell in love with some stranger on the boat," they whispered. The news caused a stir, if not quite a scandal.

Despite the fact that he was too young to know what love was, my father felt happy for his sister. Her love match left a deep impression on him because he told me the story several times. I like to think that his attachment to the story revealed his romantic side.

Young Dan and Dorothy settled in New Jersey and Dan became a successful car dealer. Together with their children, Elenka and Dan Jr., they lived the American dream, but they never forgot where they came from and always helped their family.

Back in Czechoslovakia, squeezed by the shortages of the mismanaged economy by the Communist government, we were the benefactors of Dan and Dorothy's success and their generosity. My mother counted on the supply of sugar that would come from America each year before Christmas, allowing her to bake Christmas cookies for us. She marveled at its whiteness and how small the grains of the American sugar were compared to our rough, brown version.

Every Christmas, we received two large parcels from Dorothy and Dan. One was full of food, the other was full of clothing, and it was that second parcel that we, the children, awaited with great anticipation and excitement. When the parcel finally did arrive, we all gathered in our kitchen/living room. The parcel would sit in the middle of the table and we would wait impatiently for the magic show to begin.

My mother would pull out each item separately, and give it to whom she deemed to be the right recipient. One day a leather jacket made an appearance. This was a very special gift and both my brothers wanted it. But as per the unwritten rule, the older sibling was the benefactor. My younger brother's tears were as genuine as was his happiness when at the bottom of the parcel, my mother found a second leather jacket! Although I was never in the running for the leather jacket, it stayed in my mind. It represented a dream that was achievable.

I will forever regret that I never met my aunt Dorka. I did meet the formidable Uncle Dan, but by then my aunt had passed away and I was told by the closest members of the family that I hadn't met the real Uncle Dan. He was never the same without his wife. She was the rock that kept the big guy upright.

In my heart I will always hold on to that mystical leather jacket that to me is America.

Dorka visiting her parents from US and her grown up brother, my dad

the power of the violin

Throughout history, powerful neighbors occupied the land on which stood the Soviet-dominated Czechoslovakia of my youth. Its people had a long history of pain and heartbreak. The Soviet occupation was nothing new. Perhaps it was the ability to put our pain and joy into stories and music that helped us survive even the cruelest occupations.

Most of our electricity was hydraulic and was supplied by the rivers that run from the mountains in the north toward the valleys in the south. In the winter, when the rivers froze and with it our electricity, we would gather around the large wood-burning stove, the heartbeat of our family. A single candle on the wooden table provided flickering light and added mystery or nostalgia to the tale in progress. As a child, I looked forward to those nights. My mother often invoked music in her stories. The violin, in particular, steered in her deep emotions. I often thought it would have been nice if one of her children learned to play the instrument that had such a deep meaning for her.

My father did try to make a violinist out of me. At the age of six, the earliest a parent could enroll a child in music lessons provided by the Communist government, my father did so. Not long after the instructions began, the teacher told my father I could not continue in his class. "The child is completely tone deaf," he said.

Undaunted, my father hired a private teacher. After all, how could the Communist teacher be trusted? My father's hatred of the Communists was so fierce, he could not see that the teacher might not like the Communists either but loved teaching music.

After a long year, a long, long year for me, my father asked the teacher to enroll me for the next year. The teacher looked uncomfortable while I stood within earshot, petrified. "Your daughter has a rhythm," said the teacher. "Clearly, she can hear the music; she just cannot reproduce it. I cannot take your money anymore." Thus ended my short musical career. But I never forgot the teacher's words: "She can hear the music..."

From then on, instead of fearing music, I took it into my heart, and I embraced it. Through joy, sadness, and when I needed strength or courage, music helped me. But the violin carved a special place in my heart. Not just because I heard it every day in our house; the violin had rescued me from feeling inferior and allowed me to understand its sound. Although the lone candle on our wooden table had long since been extinguished, the story my mother told us more than once, the story of my Uncle Martin and the sound of his violin, will live inside me forever.

My mother, Emilia, was not quite ten years old when my Uncle Martin left for the New World. He was one of the many thousands of emigrants who left their homes hoping for a better life.

The tiny village where my grandmother Katarina and her five children lived, consisted of twenty-five houses scattered at the foot of a small mountain. Food came from a patch of land supplemented by the surrounding hills in the form of wild berries, mushrooms, and small wild animals such as rabbits.

Grandmother Katarina became a single mother long before the term would be coined. She did the best she could for her children.

The day my Uncle Martin was leaving his home for that faraway place, my mother started to cry as soon as she woke up. She was a skinny child with short, cropped hair, which at the time was highly unusual because the tradition demanded long braids. But Grandmother Katarina was a practical woman, and she had no time for long braids. She had taken her scissors and cut off my mother's hair.

Martin was tall, slim, and looked as if he wasn't done growing. Although the closest Lutheran church was three villages over, and Grandmother Katarina did not attend often, the word about her son leaving for America got around. In his donation box, the minister found a pair of "city" pants and a jacket for Martin. The pants were black and quite threadbare, but the minister believed they would help Martin blend in better where he was going than the linen pants he had. The shoes, donated by a kind friend, were too big, but an extra pair of socks solved the problem.

"You'll be glad to have a few extra pairs of socks in America," Katarina told her son. His shirt was a traditional Slovak shirt, richly embroidered on the chest. His sister Katka had made it for him.

"Promise me you will come back." She hugged him for the last time and made herself busy, so he would not see her sorrow.

Grandma Katarina and her oldest daughter, Katka, were known in the valley that encompassed theirs and several other villages for their beautiful embroidery work. The two women worked late into the night to make clothes to sell, to save money for Martin's journey to America.

Martin had a soft spot for his little sister Emilia, and he asked his mother to let her come with them to the railway station to see him off. Grandmother agreed in hopes that the girl would stop her relentless crying. The closest train station was two hours away on foot, but a kind neighbor had offered to take them there in his cart.

Katka and her two brothers, Juraj and Jan, stood at the edge of the dusty road and kept waving long after the cart had disappeared out of sight.

The tired-looking neighbor sat on the wooden bench, holding the reins of an equally tired-looking horse, as they

Martin

climbed the hilly road toward their destination. The sad trio of mother, daughter, and departing son sat on the hay in the back of the open cart. They moved slowly through the familiar valley and its quiet, rolling fields. In the middle of summer, the gentle hills seemed to be painted many different shades of green. By September, the valley would become ablaze in rich shades of yellow, orange, and red. By the time they turned brown, the harvest would be done.

A soft wind stroked the young girl's face as her beloved brother took out his violin and started to play. The song, "Ked sa Slovak od sve vlasti odberal," spoke of a son leaving his home and family for an unfamiliar world. The violin's weeping sound confirmed the pain and sadness, and fear of a young man going to an uncertain future.

The little girl's crying echoed in the empty station long after the train's last car carrying her brother away had disappeared. The tired neighbor sat patiently on a bench and smoked his pipe. At last, the sobbing girl was willing to admit that she could no longer see the train and stepped back onto the cart that seemed large in its emptiness.

"I will never forget you, Martin," she sobbed into her mother's ample bosom, as the cart shook them gently from side to side. The way back was mostly downhill, so they arrived home before dark.

Martin found work in the Pennsylvania mines. His letters were short and not too informative. My mother suspected that due to the lack of education, his ability to write was limited. Work in the mines was hard and dangerous. Martin met an American girl and married her. He did not say much about his family, and his letters got increasingly infrequent. Years later, Martin did send us a picture of his son, Melvin, at his confirmation, and one year he told us he had a daughter, Nancy, who got married in March. I always remembered that because the phrase rhymes in Slovak. ("*Naša Nancy vydala sa v Marci.*")

There was a sizeable Slovak community in Pennsylvania, and Martin would play his violin at weddings and funerals. Not for money. They were all friends, and they were all poor.

I was about the same age my mother was when Martin left for America when my mother received a letter from Martin. He told my mother that he had tuberculosis and could not work anymore. Not long after that, my mother received her final letter from America. Inside was a death certificate and a photograph of a man lying in an open casket, dressed in a well-worn jacket, with his hands crossed on his chest, holding a bible. He was fifty years old. My mother held the photograph to her chest and wept quietly.

I watched her open the bottom drawer of her night table— "the funeral drawer," where she kept all that she needed for any given funeral. Inside, folded neatly was a black sweater, black blouse, black skirt, and black scarf. She put the photograph gently back into the envelope it arrived in and laid it on a bed of black nylon stockings at the front, right corner of the drawer.

With it, she laid down her hope to hear Martin play his violin ever again. With a heavy sigh, she closed the drawer.

When I left home, many years later, I was haunted by the fear that the only thing left from my life would be a photograph of me in a casket.

But I had more luck than my Uncle Martin had. After the Velvet Revolution booted the Soviets out of the country, I could afford to go home. Eventually, I took my whole family to meet their Slovak family.

Martin's daughter, Nancy

I am now a US citizen, and although people still ask me where I came from after a mere hello, I am no longer afraid.

But the sound of the violin still reminds me that just because I cannot sing, I am not deaf. My ears are fine-tuned to the immigrant stories of today, and my heart weeps.

Power of the Violin was published by *Potato Soup Journal* and later selected for their print anthology *Best of 2020,* still available on Amazon.

encounter with the future

In a shabby one-room school, a scrawny little boy walked slowly toward the teacher's desk, hoping to delay the inevitable punishment. The teacher stood in front of his desk and in his right hand held a long, thin piece of wood, which made a swish in the air just before it hit its target. He was tapping it softly on his left palm, as if to test its agility. He eyed the boy and said in a cruel, cold voice: "You are getting two extra whips for walking slow."

The boy shivered and sped up. As he had been taught, he offered his hand, fingers gathered together like a rosebud, exposing the soft, unprotected tips of his fingers to the cruelty of the wooden whip. He was not sure whether it was harder to withstand the pain or to suppress the tears. Letting the tears appear in front of the teacher meant further punishment.

The teacher was dressed in the latest "hussar" fashion. His trousers were tucked in his boots, which were polished to perfection. His hair, glistening with pomade, looked dark against the white collar that peeked out of his tight jacket. The jacket was held even tighter at the waist with a wide belt, a belt he was not shy about using. Many children had the scars to attest to it. His mustache was twisted upward at the ends, and the boy could see his lips curled in an ugly smile.

"This will help you walk faster." The teacher hit the boy twice.

"This will help you remember that you are Hungarian and to speak Hungarian instead of local gibberish." He raised the whip and hit the boy's fingers hard three times.

The boy managed to control his tears, but when he sat on the hard, wooden bench, he could feel that his pants were wet.

The year was 1910, and the place was a little village called Myjava, which belonged to the Hungarian part of the Austro-Hungarian Empire. The punishment for speaking Slovak was swift and certain. The little boy's name was Jan and he did learn to speak Hungarian, but when Slovakia became part of the newly formed Czechoslovakia in 1918, he vowed never to speak it again.

Sixty years later, Jan sat on another hard, wooden bench. The place was Victoria Station in London. Fear, less ominous but equally imminent, was descending on his bent, tired shoulders.

He had traveled from Czechoslovakia to see his daughter, who lived in London. Excited to see her, Jan was one of the first to get off the train. A crowd gathered behind the gate as people waited for their loved ones to appear. A few times, Jan thought that he spotted his daughter, but it turned out to be someone else's child. He watched as the people started to thin out.

He found a bench not too far from where his train had arrived, in case his daughter came a bit late. He sat down and checked his

My dad is the boy sitting with the hat in front

pockets again to see if he could find the paper with his daughter's address, which his wife told him to "guard with his life." He gave up figuring out where and how he may have lost it. It was gone.

The big clock in the middle of the station said 7:00 p.m., and the crowd from the train was gone. He had to face the possibility that his daughter did not receive the last letter with his arrival time. He knew that, if she had, she would have come.

Jan watched as people hurried toward their destinations. He did not speak English, so the voices in the train station were just noise to him. As he pondered what to do, he noticed a tall young man walking toward him. Next to him walked a person who looked like an older version of the teacher that had made him wet his pants sixty years ago. His fingers tingled in memory. He was mesmerized by that vision of so long ago.

As he watched the young man walking next to his "old nemesis," Jan felt very alone and could not help feeling a bit of envy at what he assumed was their reunion. When they drew close to his bench, audible despite the hum of the station, he clearly recognized the words, "Are you thirsty, Papa?" spoken in Hungarian. Jan jumped off his bench and interrupted father and son.

"Please can you help me? My daughter and I missed each other and I don't know how to find a train to get to her." He had not spoken Hungarian in decades and was surprised how much he still remembered. The young man stopped, looked at his father, and told him to sit on the bench the stranger had just vacated.

"Don't move, Papa," the young man said to his father, "I don't want to lose you."

Then he turned to the stranger and asked, "Where does your daughter live?"

"Ipswich," said Jan, thinking there was no point telling the stranger the whole story about the lost address.

The young man frowned. "That is a long way from London. Are you sure she is not here?"

"I don't know, but I do know how to get to her in Ipswich," Jan said with a tired look.

"All right." The young man realized that the man before him had probably endured the same long train journey across Europe that his own father had made.

"Do you have money for the train to Ipswich?" he asked kindly.

"Yes." Jan reached into his breast pocket and gave the young man a white envelope with English money.

When they reached the ticket window, the young man counted the money and realized that the stranger was short by a few shillings. He bought Jan the ticket, making up the difference with his own money. Then he put Jan on the train, which stood not far from where he had left his own father. Jan thanked the young man in his best Hungarian and they shook hands.

It was the first time he had willingly shaken hands with a Hungarian, let alone with genuine gratitude. Jan was still waving to the young man from the window of the train when the older man joined his son on the platform. Jan watched them walking away when, suddenly, the older man turned around and hurried toward Jan's window. Jan could hear his heart pound in what he knew to be an irrational fear, but he continued to stand up. The older man handed him a small travel bag through the window.

"My son said you have a long way to go," he said, as he handed Jan a small parcel. "Take this. My wife always packs too much."

"Thank you very much," said Jan. He watched father and son talking and gesticulating as people who have not seen each other for a long time tend to do. He understood. How ironic, he thought, that the language that was literally "beat into him" would help him so many years later.

He let the tears roll freely on his wrinkled cheeks. He closed his eyes as if to bar the painful image of the past from his memory. He took a handkerchief out of his coat pocket and dried his eyes.

"Today I got food," he said aloud and opened the bag that the Hungarian had handed him just moments before. "Ah, a salami sandwich, green paprika, and small bottle of red wine." He smiled and bit into the sandwich with gusto.

As the train pulled out of the Victoria train station, night fell on London, but Jan felt lightness in his heart, beyond the satisfaction of his stomach.

The young woman stood by the gate marked "Trains from Dover." She strained to see her father. Her lips were still smiling as she anticipated greeting her father, but her eyes started to fill with tears and her heart beat loudly in fear. Is he going to be the last off the train, she wondered, more in hope than annoyance. The last passenger had passed her and the train pulled out of the station.

Suddenly, a terrible idea crossed her mind. What if my father fell asleep and the train goes...where? She ran to the information booth but was reassured by two separate employees that the conductor walks through the train more than once before the train is allowed to leave the station. They told her to speak to the station's police.

"There is no passenger list, miss," said the police officer.

"Can you call the border and see if my father arrived in England?" she pleaded, her voice laden with sobs.

"No, miss, there are hundreds of people working at the border. How can I know whom to call? No, there is no central list."

The senior policeman, a former bobby, felt sorry for the distraught young woman.

"Are you sure you have the right date, miss?" he asked kindly. "Do you have your father's letter with you?"

She did not, but the idea that she had made a mistake and that it was the wrong day for her father's arrival gave her hope. Sitting on the Tube on the way home, it was this hope that kept her from descending into panic.

Decades passed before I was able to smile at this memory. My father came to London so that he could be there for my twenty-first birthday. Today is my father's birthday. He would have been 105 years old. I moved across the pond to New York City long ago and I still miss him. As I am remembering my worry all those years ago in London, my cell phone rings. It is my daughter. We are having our mother-daughter lunch, so she called to make sure that I have the right place and time. I put the phone close to my heart and, holding it tight, I still remember.

After a frantic night, my father and I did connect the next morning. He may have lost my London address, but he was able to find the house where I had previously lived in Ipswich. He had been there with me on that fateful day two years earlier, on August 22, 1968, when the Soviet Union invaded Czechoslovakia. Not surprisingly, the place had stayed etched in my father's memory. Brian, who still lived in the house and with whom I kept in touch, drove my father to London. I thanked my friend profusely, but was sad that I could not thank the two kind men who helped my father at the railway station.

"Every time you help a stranger," my father reassured me, "you will thank them." I let that guide my life.

What had happened? At the time, trains coming from the "Continent" arrived at a separate part of the train station. At the border, all passengers had to disembark and go through border control and customs inspection, carrying their suitcases. My father went to get a drink of water and found himself at the domestic side of the train station at Dover, where he had crossed into England. It did not occur to him that it would matter which train he took as long as the sign said it was going to London's Victoria station. By the time the policeman and I checked the domestic side "just in case," it was 8:00 p.m. and my father was on his way to Ipswich.

For my father the episode had a far-reaching consequence. The kindness of complete strangers undermined his resentment and erased the old pain he had carried with him from youth. His decision to leave the painful history in the past both healed and liberated him.

"Sometimes memory is our enemy," he said to me. "It can teach people not to trust each other. Even worse, seek revenge."

I often wondered, if there were a scale to show how much evil we have learned to avoid from history, as opposed to how much anger and distrust and revenge we carry forward from it, which way would the scale tip?

I am the first to arrive for the lunch with my daughter. I ask for a table next to the window. One of the best things about New York City is people-watching. There is a story inside each person who walks by. Watching strangers makes me feel as if I am in a library full of books in progress.

I see my daughter walking toward the restaurant. Tall, athletic, she walks with the confidence of a young woman who knows who she is, what she wants, and is willing to work to achieve it.

"Hello, Mum, I have something to tell you." That's my daughter. She gets to the point. "I met a boy, a while ago, actually, and I really like him." I wait because I know her well enough to know that she is not finished. "I think he might be a keeper."

"Well," I say, noncommittal, "I look forward to meeting him."

"You will like him," she says with certainty. "His father is Hungarian. I know that you will have a lot in common."

For a brief moment I think about getting back the money I paid for her education, but I smile instead and say, "You are right; we were neighbors in Europe."

No history. My father would be pleased.

Encounter with the Future was published by bioStories and nominated for a **Pushcart Prize.** Published in the fall issue, 2020.

dream on ice

Rummaging through the storage places in my basement as I looked for a brochure I had lent to my son when he was in high school, I came across an essay he wrote, I am guessing, at age twelve:

> "Most of my life I have lived in America and have all my needs that I could possibly want satisfied. Recently, I got a dose of what life is like in other countries. My cousin arrived from Slovakia to stay with us and at first glance, he loved everything about America. I mean when my mum bought him hockey skates (his were from the Ice Age) he slept with them. But then he asked, 'Why do people in America never turn off the lights? What a waste...'"

My nephew Palo's skates were old, although not quite "Ice Age." My brother, who was still in Czechoslovakia, at that time still under the Soviet thumb, certainly could not afford the fancy skates I bought for his son, whose dream was to play in the NHL. He was not the first, nor would he be the last, young boy dreaming about fame on ice. Before the fall of the Soviet Union, the NHL was littered with Eastern European hockey players. For a long time, it was their ticket out from behind the Iron Curtain and into freedom.

The skates and the hockey brought me back to my own childhood, in the old Czechoslovakia, where skating in the winter was kind of like breathing. We skated on the frozen streets when we were very young. We did not have to worry about traffic, nobody had cars, and the occasional horse-drawn cart was more worried about us spooking the horse with the puck than the other way around.

As we got older, we graduated to skating on the nearby pond. "Nearby" was a relative description as it was two kilometers away through open fields where the wind threatened to blow us away. There was of course no transportation, and ice, snow, and wind ruled out bicycles. There were several ponds in the area known as Kamenny Mlyn (Stone Mill). It derived its name from a real mill that had stopped being functional many years earlier.

The main lake where we swam in the summer was deep and seldom froze completely, but when it did, the ice was superior to all the other lakes. Rumor had it that there was a warm spring under the lake, and we were forbidden to skate there, told time and time again to stick to the smaller, shallower lakes.

But the lure of the ice on the big lake was irresistible to the boys. It was black and smooth and fast. Just as important, there were no branches sticking out of the ice, tripping the boys focused on the puck.

I was an only girl in our neighborhood full of boys, so my brothers had the unenviable task of taking me with them whenever they wanted to go to Kamenny Mlyn to play hockey. I dreamed of being a figure skater and hoped to peel off one of my brothers to skate with me, à la the 1962 world champion brother-and-sister team of Eva and Pavel Roman. Of course, I had a better chance of going around the world with Gagarin in his Sputnik than I had to dance on ice with either of my brothers.

Still, I persevered. One day I was practicing my pirouette while the boys were playing an intense hockey game against their neighborhood rival team when the puck just missed me, rocketed past at an alarming speed, and stopped on some ice of dubious strength. The boys came over toward my side of the lake and huddled together discussing the best way to retrieve the puck.

It was something none of them were willing to sacrifice. At the beginning of the winter, each boy received a supply of pucks for the season from their parents, and if they lost them all, there would not be another puck available until the next winter. It was getting warmer, and spring was not far off, so the puck supply was at its lowest. But the boys still hoped for a few more games, and nobody wanted to lose the precious commodity.

The side of the lake that was most exposed to the sun had already begun to melt. We all knew not to get too close to that side, but the puck did not, and had stopped on the thin ice.

"You are the smallest and the lightest," my oldest brother, Jan, said to me. "You have to go get the puck."

"I will, if you sign up for figure skating with me," I countered. I wasn't going to risk my life for just a puck.

The boys huddled together again and after some gesticulations, they let me know my answer by turning their backs on me and skating away. I watched them take off their scarves and tie them together. Then my brother Pavel, holding the rope of scarves with one hand, slowly approached the runaway puck. The rest of the boys watched in silence.

Pavel got within reach of the puck, stretched his hand to grab it, when without warning the ice broke and he was waist-deep in the water. The rest of the boys started to pull on the rope of scarves, but the ice kept breaking.

"Lie flat!" shouted one of the boys, not easily achieved since the heavy skates kept Pavel's feet down. But he did hang on to the scarf and attempted to kick his feet to get himself into a horizontal position. I looked on, terrified.

My brother Jan lay down on the ice and inched closer to Pavel while another boy held on to his skates and another held that boy's waist. Slowly they pulled Pavel out of the water. Wet, frightened, but with great pride, Pavel produced the puck from inside his jacket.

There was no further discussion. We all knew what we had to do; change into our shoes and jog all the way home. The warmer weather that had started to melt the lake and Pavel's body heat from running prevented his clothing freezing on him.

The punishment for disobeying the order not to skate on the big lake loomed large over my brothers' heads, allowing me to extract the promise of figure skating lessons from both of them as a payment for my silence.

Unfortunately, the weather turned warm and there was no more ice time for any of us. Although the rescued puck would keep its value for the next winter season, the power of my blackmail threat did not. The following year, my brothers reneged on their promise to skate with me, but it no longer mattered because during the summer I got involved in swimming, and skating with my brothers lost its allure.

* * *

I looked down at my son's essay and put it back in its folder. I forgot about the brochure I came to find, but I made sure to turn off the lights.

Dream on Ice was published by *Ariel Chart International Literary Journal*, in its May 2, 2021 issue.

cosmic painter

My brother Jan, I always felt, was the writing talent in the family. But he was much too self-critical and I suspect far shyer than he, even now, would admit. My mother, the "steam engine" behind her children, never missed an opportunity to grow her children's talent.

Jan wrote a poem that his teacher felt was very good and she submitted it to a local competition. The poem won and it was forwarded to the regional round, where Jan would have to perform it himself in front of the judges and an audience. Jan refused to do it. The teacher, who happened to also be my brother Pavel's teacher, agreed with my mother's plan to have Pavel, who thrived in the spotlight, to perform the poem and they would simply put down "by Kocvara" without the first name. I went with my mother to see Pavel perform; predictably, Jan refused to join us.

The poem won and Pavel was invited to talk to the panel about the poem, which exposed the scheme, and the second-place poem received the diploma and the recognition.

My mother and the teacher received a reprimand but that was all.

Ironically, later, in his adult life, in England and the USA, Jan would make his living by writing and reading his work both at the BBC and the Voice of America.

For my children, the highlight of my brother Jan's visit would always be to listen to his stories, especially after he had a beer or two. The following is the story I begged him to write, as he was there and I was not, but I did not fare any better than his mother and his teacher. His answer was always the same: "You write it." And so, I did.

* * *

What follows is how I recall Jan's story.

Jan was in his third year of hotel school, and through the summer he had to clock in some practice time, which he did at the Hotel Carlton in Bratislava. Josef, Jan's coworker at the hotel, was always creative. Not always in a tangible way, but in the days when people believed that he who does not steal from the government steals from his family, his creativity often yielded him success. He believed there were two ways to succeed under the Communist regime: Join the party and sell your soul, or outsmart them. Josef was willing to sell a lot of what he owned and even what he did not have, but not his principles.

Josef had a quick mind, but he was not a good student. Books held no fascination for him unless they had a lot of pictures in them and were about America. He finished the minimal education required by the government at the age of fifteen. What he did not lack was ambition; he could never be accused of aiming low. He had an eye on the job at the best hotel in Bratislava, Hotel Carlton. He was not quite sure what he wanted to do there, but he would take any job as long as it was at the Hotel Carlton. He believed all the American success stories he had heard and was confident that he could become a millionaire as long as he did not brag about it. Of course, a million koruna and a million dollars was a different value, but to him, a million was a million. His long-term plan was still to make it to America.

Josef was likable and, thanks to his mother, who washed and ironed his clothes, he looked presentable. He was charming and what he did not know, he imagined he knew and would say it with such certainty, people believed it and seldom questioned it. He would learn later that in the US, they had a fairly colorful word for that.

Although he charmed the human resources woman at the hotel into giving him the job, he did not convince her of his management qualities. Maybe he would have if his academic papers did not undermine his argument. He was hired as cleaning staff. Before long, he knew almost every employee at the hotel. He never forgot a name, face, and position and could match each to the right person with an absolute certainty.

On his way home, he liked to stop at the bar opposite the hotel where he would visualize his rise to fame. The bar was buzzing with the news about Valentina Tereshkova, the first woman who went into space. She orbited the earth, solo, forty-eight times, he read in the paper on the table, which was more than Gagarin, the first man in space.

"Of course, the Soviet Union would push the woman ahead of the man," was Josef's reaction. "What ass-kissers." He had nothing against emancipation, but he did not like to have his nose rubbed in it.

Within two months, Josef knew about every job available at the hotel and he began to scout his next job. After a weeklong deliberation, he decided that he would be an asset to the hotel working as a receptionist. He believed he spoke English because he could sing all Elvis Presley's songs, and languages were important at the reception desk. He was in a good mood when he came home.

"You promised to paint my bedroom weeks ago," complained his mother.

"I will do it tomorrow; it's my day off," he said cheerily.

"I'll believe it when I see it," replied his mother.

True to his word, the next morning Josef painted the room dark blue, then added splashes of white and yellow to bring the room up to his level of cheerfulness.

"It looks as if a bomb exploded in a paint shop!" said his mother when she saw it. "Who do you think you are? Picasso?"

His feelings hurt, he went to a bar next to the hotel where he bumped into one of his coworkers.

"Ahoj Vojto!" Josef greeted his pal. "What's new?" Vojto seemed annoyed.

"Extra work, that is what's new." He drained his beer then continued. "You will be sweating it too."

"Why?" asked Josef.

"Khrushchev, Gagarin, and Tereshkova are coming to the hotel."

"Holy shit!" Josef could not believe it.

That night, Josef could not sleep. His mother's words came back to him in the darkness. She compared him to Picasso! He realized he was too good to be a receptionist. He was a painter, an artist. Two cosmonauts were coming to his hotel. It was a sign—he was a cosmic painter. Not a cosmic painter, he was The Cosmic Painter.

Josef took a day off and went to the shop by the river Danube where they sold art supplies. He painted all night. Using every color he could afford, he sprinkled the paint all over the canvas. The two Sputniks were two blobs that appeared to spit at each other.

"That's fair competition!" he thought. By morning he had a plan.

Josef knew well the corridors of the hotel the cosmonauts would be walking through on their way to reception. Just before they would clear one of the corners, there was a cleaning closet. That was where he would spend the night in the name of art.

The night before the distinguished guests arrived, Josef settled cheerfully among brooms, brushes, and cleaning sprays. He practiced his speech in Russian, and for the first time in his life was glad that he was forced to learn the language since the second grade. He held his art close to his heart as a silent goodbye.

Tomorrow, he knew he would be famous. He dozed off more times than he would admit to himself, but finally he could see the light coming through the small crack on the side of the door. Timing was everything.

The celebrated guests were accompanied by officials and scores of journalists. There was an absence of security around the distinguished guests. After all, they were visiting their brothers, not a gun-toting country like America. The TV lights gave Josef a sufficient heads-up.

He brushed his hair in the gray light of the closet, straightened the jacket he had his mother iron to perfection, then stepped out of his closet with his painting in hand, just in time before the first cameras turned the corner. Since the camera operators were walking backward, at first, they did not notice Josef standing in the middle of the corridor with a broad smile and wearing what he deemed an artist's hat.

As soon as Gagarin rounded the corner with Tereshkova at his side, Josef put the painting into Gagarin's hands and shook bewildered Tereshkova's hand. He stopped the moving delegation with a loud proclamation at the beginning of his speech. "I am a Wassily Kandinsky disciple…"

The security looked at the hotel manager, who had a blank look on his face. Silence fell on the group and Josef's words dedicating the painting were heard on television and quickly jotted down by all the press. Cameras flashed and the unprepared cosmonauts managed a thank-you that seemed sincere.

The Cosmic Painter and his painting were all over the newspapers the following morning, until someone pointed out to the hotel manager that this fellow was in fact a janitor at the hotel.

Josef's fame was short-lived, although he argued that a janitor could be an artist. His claim was taken to the Communist organization of artists, who deemed him completely devoid of talent. Nobody knows what happened to the painting.

Josef remained a janitor until the fall of Communism, after which he made it to America, to San Francisco, where he got a job as a painter in several hotels. Eventually he started his own business painting people's homes. He was well liked and became quite successful. For an extra fee, he would paint a cosmic scene on the wall for selected customers.

He signed it: Josef, the Cosmic Painter.

olympia

An Academy with a Difference

The late-sixties London was hard to ignore. Especially for a girl who still remembered her first Christmas in the big house in Ipswich, left alone over the Christmas holiday. I remember being terrified by any sound, real or imaginary. I was saved by the prospect of the premiere of the Beatles movie *The Magical Mystery Tour*. I counted the days and when the big day came, unlike many critics, I was not disappointed. The MMT, as I would affectionately call it, influenced me deeply and for the first time I felt some semblance of a confidence, or perhaps it was a permission, to dream. When later Mrs. Landis told me I should be a model, not an occupation I had even heard of while home in Czechoslovakia, I let it linger in my mind.

The reality of being a model came from the most unexpected place: the office of Claude Hornby & Cox, the solicitor firm where I was working. It was Monday morning in fall, my favorite time of year, when Mr. Cox put a newspaper page on my table saying, "You should enter." *The Daily Mail* newspaper was holding a competition to find ten international models who would participate at the Olympia's New Year Show.

I sent in my photograph thinking, "How hard can it be?" After all, my father used me as his model whenever he needed to fit clothes for a person who was my size. I had never heard the expression "fit model" or "catwalk model," let alone knew the difference.

Within three weeks I received an invitation to come to the London Academy of Modeling on Bond Street. I washed my hair and put on my best blouse.

When I arrived, I saw beautiful girls wearing mini dresses and makeup. I turned to leave but I was stopped by a man who was walking behind me.

"Where are you going?" he asked.

"Oh, I made a mistake."

"I don't think you did. You just feel intimidated," he said. "Stay."

I stayed partially because he was blocking my exit and partially because it felt good to be encouraged, and I was curious to see how far off Mrs. Landis was in her suggestion.

The day turned out to be a very long day. Out of 800 entrees to the newspaper, sixty girls were invited for a personal appearance. There were many rounds before the panel narrowed it to the last ten, who would be the lucky winners and would participate in the live fashion show. After each round I was sure I would be eliminated in the next one. I could not believe when I was one of the last ten girls standing on the catwalk.

SATURDAY, DECEMBER 7, 1968

Meet the models

. . . at the
New Year
Show

The day I became a model

The win came with a comprehensive modeling course at the London Academy of Modeling. Yes, there was such a thing. The course was very useful for a tomboy like me who always had to keep up with her older brothers. We learned how to walk, depending on what we were wearing. There were the necessary makeup lessons; we learned how to get out of a sports car gracefully in a mini dress. How to use hotel restrooms to check appearance before an audition. (You walked confidently past the doorman with the eyes fixed on some painting in the distance at the same time scanning the signs for Ladies room or WC.)

The man who would not let me leave turned out to be the photographer who told us about lighting and shadows and the many ways to get the best out of the camera, some of which I use till this day.

Once the show started, I discovered quickly the difference between my father's brand of modeling, which was "stand still so I can fit the dress on you," and a fashion show with its furious-but-precise pace, blinding lights, and blaring music.

The Olympia fashion show lasted fourteen straight days and I was paid four pounds a day (no difference for Sunday, which some complained about but to me, was an absolute fortune).

Many celebrities came to the show, which was broadly covered by all newspapers, and I found myself being photographed with many famous people. But nothing surpassed being photographed with the World Cup trophy the English soccer team recently won. My brothers were soccer fanatics, so when I was chosen to be one of the three girls to be photographed holding the trophy, they were ecstatic.

After the show ended, I briefly dated Emperor Rosco, whom I met at Olympia. His real name was, and I believe he still uses it,

Michael Pasternak. I could not believe I was dating one of the disc jockeys on Radio Caroline that used to keep my spirits up when I came to Ipswich. It felt very unreal to me. Our friendship was brief, yet long enough to make me reread *Doctor Zhivago*, in Russian, no less. I do not think Michael Pasternack is related to the famous Russian author Boris Pasternack, but then I never asked.

I also graduated from the YWCA to an apartment in Baron's Court. I still had to share a bedroom with two other girls, but we had our own kitchen, bathroom, and—most exciting of all—our very own living room.

My new roommates had gone home for the holidays, so on New Year's Eve 1968, I had the place all to myself. Over Birds Eye fish sticks, mashed potatoes, and peas, I awaited the arrival of the New Year. I thought that I had reason to be hopeful. I was reasonably proficient in English, and I could support myself financially. I was confident in my ability to handle unpredictable events. I had learned a lot about myself in the past year and believed I was wiser, more mature—even if I did have Babycham (low-alcohol sparkling pear cider) in my glass.

My optimism was also fueled by a recent photo session with Barry, the photographer who had taught the modeling course at the London Academy of Modeling. The models needed pictures for their portfolios, and the photographers had their own portfolio to keep updated.

"You don't pay me, and I don't pay you," Barry explained to me over the telephone. "We both get what we need."

When I asked why he chose me, he replied, "I figured you were most likely to need free photos."

I liked his perception and his honesty. We became friends. Barry was married and lived in Enfield, a suburb of London, with his wife and their infant daughter. He was also an assistant to Norman Parkinson, which allowed him to use one of the studios at *Vogue* magazine where he took many of the photographs for my first portfolio. I dreamed one day my photograph would be on the cover of *Vogue*. Alas, that was not to be, but my photograph did appear on *Vogue*'s inside pages.

The photos turned out well, and Barry got me a few jobs. Understanding that I could not be a freelance model at the time because I needed steady income, he suggested I look for a job at the wholesale house as a showroom model. Which was what I did.

My mother's health was holding up and my brothers planned to come to London in the summer. The spring seemed more beautiful than ever as I walked down Park Lane on Sundays. I would smile at everyone. I felt I was on top of the world. The Beatles-Rolling Stones rivalry was invented by newspapers, but my loyalty skewed toward the Bee Gees.

The summer of 1969 was relatively carefree. In Czechoslovakia, Alexander Dubcek was still in government and, although largely powerless, he did his best to slow down the inevitable tightening of the Soviet yoke. The border was yet to close. For those like my brothers, who'd applied for their exit visa early, travel was still possible.

I found my brothers jobs at a restaurant owned by Mr. Kovach, who was originally from Bratislava. I arranged a room for them at the YMCA halfway between the restaurant and my flat.

My roommates got married during the summer and the girls who replaced them were different. My job at the fashion house was complicated by the fact that one of my bosses did not like me. But my brothers' presence made up for all my problems and we had a wonderful time. We hitchhiked to Liverpool to pay homage to the Beatles and FC Liverpool. My brothers could not take the time off together, so I went twice. We had a small Czechoslovak flag that we made ourselves and every time we waved it, we got a ride. People were incredibly kind to us and often went out of their way to deliver us to the next best spot for our journey and most of the time we got fed as well.

I got tickets for the Bee Gees concert at the Royal Albert Hall. I went to see if I could get an autograph and once again when the security heard I was from Czechoslovakia, they let me into the press area. I will never know what got into me, but I said to the man who just walked out of the dressing room, "I am a journalist from Czechoslovakia and I would like to interview Barry Gibb for my Czechoslovak Youth paper."

The kind man actually went to enquire if Barry Gibb had the time to talk to me. I panicked. I knew enough about journalism that I could not fake it since I did not even have a paper and pencil. I left before the kind man returned and I will never know if Barry Gibb agreed to the "interview."

And then there was that bittersweet Rolling Stones concert in Hyde Park after the tragic death of Brian Jones. The concert was both sad and electrifying. I will never forget it. Mick Jagger wore that famous fem white shirt and if he was high, I would not blame him.

In September, I waved goodbye to my brothers, and to the carefree time that would never return in quite such an abundance. "Those were the days..."

finley's gift

Nobody, least of all me, could have imagined that Eros, whose statue is mounted atop the Shaftesbury Memorial Fountain in Piccadilly Circus, would pierce my heart before the year was over.

The fountain beneath the statue often served as my perch, from which I liked to observe people. The imaginary complications of strangers helped to shrink my own troubles.

"Hello, what are you doing here?"

I was not sure if the question was for me, but the voice sounded familiar. It brought me back to reality. I looked up to see the tall, slim figure of a young man I recognized from work. His black hair was cut short and he wore black-rimmed glasses. I thought that his jeans and blue, oxford-striped shirt was an odd combo, but he looked handsome.

He sat next to me, uninvited. His name was Finley, and we talked about work first, but before long, he segued into his fiancée,

Amanda. He told me he had just broken off the engagement, and he felt terrible about it.

"Better now than later," I said.

But Finley was not looking for advice. What he needed was to ease his guilt by explaining his reasons. I was perfect for the role. Not a total stranger, but not a friend to either party. But men can talk about their emotions only so long. Soon, we moved to other topics. It turned out that Finley lived only a few streets away from me in West London. I learned that our birthdays were only one day apart, though Finley was five years older. I also learned that although he was born in England, his family recently moved to Canada. When it got dark, we took the Tube back together.

"Why were you sitting at the fountain in Piccadilly? Were you waiting for someone?" he asked unexpectedly.

"Long story," I replied.

"Perhaps someday you will tell me."

"Perhaps," I said.

Finley and I became friends. On weekends, we liked to go to the movies, and we often wandered around London, stopping by the pub for some Ploughman's Lunch. He was easy to talk to and, in some ways, he, too, was leading a temporary existence. He was not sure if he was going to stay in England or join his family in Canada. Our friendship grew deeper, though not romantic.

It was the end of the sixties, and London was ablaze with color and pop music. Young people played guitar and sang all over the city, occasionally squatting in empty buildings. Pop stars were arrested for smoking pot on a regular basis, and Mary Quant would cut the skirts so short that the false eyelashes the girls were wearing often seemed longer than the hemline.

Despite my mini success in winning the *Find the Next*

International Model competition, I knew I could not afford to be a freelance model. I also suspected that the fact that I was from Czechoslovakia had played in my favor. My confidence was not exactly sky high. After all, I came from a country where emancipation was hammered into girls' heads from a very early age and where looks were nothing to be proud of.

Finley and I, and his now ex-fiancée, worked at one of the many wholesale fashion houses. I was hired as a showroom model. I would show the samples for important clients like Selfridges. When I was not needed as a model, my job was to sell dresses from the stock to clients who only had one or two boutiques.

There were several bosses and one of them, Rod, hated me. He always referred to me as a "Commie" and belittled me at every opportunity. I tolerated his insults because I knew the job for me was temporary, and the pay was good.

During the spring, both of my original roommates got married and moved out. Each girl was responsible for finding a replacement for herself. The flaw in this plan was that the departing girl did not have to live with her own replacement. My new roommates, Clara and Kristy, were very different from the girls they were replacing. They were younger, hipper, and smoked constantly.

The atmosphere within the flat changed dramatically. We did not have a TV, so I would come home to find loud music and clouds of smoke rising up toward the ceiling, whenever Clara and Kristy were around. They listened to Jethro Tull, Jimi Hendrix, and Janis Joplin. Clara was the first to move in. I got on with her well enough, until Kristy arrived. After that, life at the flat changed.

Clara and Kristy became inseparable. Kristy had beautiful, straight hair that reached below her waist. She was sullen and she never smiled. I never knew what kind of work she did, only that she hated it. From their perspective, they found me "square." They made fun of me because I liked *The Prime of Miss Jean Brodie*. Clara did try to make life at the flat amicable, but clearly Kristy and I were different people.

By September the atmosphere in the flat had become as unpleasant as the smoke-filled air, which came from other sources as well as cigarettes. It was during one of those self-exiled evenings that I first met Finley.

Between the atmosphere at work and at the flat, I spent a lot of time sitting at Piccadilly Circus. Just as I thought things could not get worse, I received devastating news from home. After the Soviets Union put a bloody end to Prague Spring, the iron grip from Moscow got tighter. All Czechoslovakian citizens still abroad had an order to return by December 31, 1969, regardless of their visa status. The alternative was to be declared an illegal immigrant, with all its implications.

The memory of the tanks rolling down Wenceslas Square made me shiver.

You have a difficult decision in front of you, wrote my father. *It would not be easy for us to not be able to see you. But it would not be easy to watch you be unhappy. You must make your decision, whether you stay in England or come back home, without regard to us. No matter what you decide to do, we will support you, we will always love you.*

If I were to stay in England, I may never see my family again. My brothers would have a hard time getting jobs if their sister was an illegal emigrant. My father was to retire that year and it was doubtful he would get his full pension under those circumstances.

And then there was my mother. She was in remission, but I knew there was no cure for her cancer. If her condition were to worsen, I would not be able to go and see her. If I went home, what if some petty local official decided to label me a traitor just to enhance his own standing? I could not shake the image of my father, bent over his sewing machine, foot on the pedal, going, going, going, endlessly sewing. My brave, angry, gentle father. He could not prevent the albatross landing on my shoulders after all.

At work, I was preoccupied and, of course, we were very busy with small-scale customers buying Christmas stock for their boutiques. Rod was on a warpath that day and had been nitpicking at me from the moment I arrived. I finished helping a customer and I was looking forward to my lunch break. I handed Rod the paperwork. I was walking out of the showroom when I heard him yelling at me.

"You stupid foreigner, you incompetent idiot!"

He told me I should be a housemaid and scrub toilets, since that was all I was capable of. I did not stop to find out what mistake I made. I walked out of the showroom and kept on walking.

I reached Oxford Street, barely managing to keep my tears in check. I walked through Hyde Park, and I headed toward the flat. Slowly, I regained my feelings, and I began to laugh. With all I had to deal with, I was concerned about Rod being unfair? The tanks in Prague were unfair. Orders to go back home to a hostile and unknown environment was unfair. My mother having cancer was unfair.

On the other hand, not having a job would eat up my savings that I wanted to bring home. And that, too, was unfair. I allowed myself to hate Rod. I opened the door to my flat just as the phone started to ring.

"I better take you out and feed you since you're unemployed," said Finley.

"Thanks," I answered.

I was glad to go out so that I didn't have to face my roommates or spend money on food. But, more than that, I needed to talk to someone. I felt alone and afraid. I'd told Finley before that it was a long story. That evening I filled in the blanks.

He was sympathetic: "You poor bugger; you're screwed either way."

The next morning, with no job to go to, I took the Tube to Piccadilly. It was past rush hour as I watched people walking aimlessly, looking around and taking photographs. Tourists. I sat at the edge of the fountain and delayed dealing with my dilemma. After all, the sun was shining, and it was my birthday. I was twenty years old that day, and so it seemed reason enough to think about happier times.

In February 1968, I was given an exit visa valid till May 1970. More than two years! The gate of life had seemed to be wide open and the future had looked bright.

But the letter from home would not let me escape into my thoughts for long. It sat folded in my pocket, heavy with its implications. I pictured life moving along without me. Nobody would notice I was gone. In London, I would no longer exist, and back home, my dream of becoming a journalist lay dead beneath the Soviet tanks.

I saw an advertisement in a local shopwindow for a job working the evening shift in a pie factory. I filled out the paperwork and was sent to the factory doctor to make sure that I carried no diseases. The shift would be from six in the evening till midnight. Perhaps leaning over a conveyor belt making minced meat pies would help me decide who to sacrifice.

When I walked into the flat, I found three envelopes on the

kitchen table. It was a notice from our landlord. We had to be out by January first. My heart sank. I felt sorry for myself with the intensity only a twenty-year-old on her birthday could muster. I cried and cried.

The doorbell rang. I looked at my watch. It was five thirty. I had to go to the pie factory. *Not the best idea to be late on the first day of work,* I thought.

Finley was standing at the door.

"What took you so long?"

"Walk with me and I'll tell you."

It was not a very long walk to the factory, and there was not much to tell. I was evicted, and I did not want to play the blame game. We walked the rest of the way in silence.

"Well, Prince Charming, this is my castle." I attempted to lighten the mood, still hiccupping from all the crying.

"You should cry more often," Finley said. "You look beautiful."

Walking up the stone stairs of the old pie factory, I thought about that odd exchange. But the overbearing smell of disinfectant soon brought my focus back to reality. I put on the apron, the hair net, and the rubber gloves that were given to me by our supervisor, then I stood with my coworkers by a conveyer belt, putting tin containers into empty slots.

We all had nametags. Looking at my nametag, my coworkers decided that I did not speak English. There was not much talking while we worked, because the belt was moving at a pretty good clip. But during the break, I did not correct my coworkers' assumptions. The last thing I wanted was to engage in a conversation about my life.

Christmas was fast approaching. The decorations in the local shops sparkled in their splendor. I bought the suitcase I would need for my journey home. Clara and Kristy had found a flat together and moved out. I had nowhere to go, and since the rent was paid till the end of the year, I stayed at the flat alone. Despite the cheeriness of Christmas, the days were short and cold. I avoided putting the half-crown coin into the gas meter to turn on the heat as much as I could.

I was getting sick of minced-meat pies—my diet five days a week since I received a free pie each night at the factory. Not wasting food was a religion ingrained in me from my earliest childhood. So even though I did not like the pies, I ate them.

I started to pack clothes into my new suitcase. I wondered if I would ever need them again. What if they put me in prison? My imagination was running unchecked, spiraling into panic. I put on a Beatles album and sang along with Ringo Star: *They gonna put me in the movies, they gonna make a big star out of me...*

The phone rang. It was Finley.

"What are you doing?"

"Packing," I said.

"So, you decided to go home." It was not a question.

I said nothing.

"You still there?"

"Yes, for now." I was fighting panic. This really was the end.

"I'll come and see you before you go to the pie factory," said Finley.

Pen in hand, I sat at the table and wrote a letter to my parents telling them I would come home. How could I enjoy freedom if I had to put those that I loved in jeopardy? I licked the envelope, sealing the letter and my future. I would mail it the next day.

I felt hollow and cold. I sat in the nearly empty living room waiting for Finley.

I ate yet another pie.

It was nearly time for me to leave for work. Something must have delayed Finley. But it no longer mattered. I'd made my decision. I opened the door and found Finley standing outside, poised to ring the doorbell. Instead of hello, he said, "I will marry you so that you can stay in England and don't have to hurt your family."

"What are you talking about?"

"I will marry you. The marriage would protect you and your family back home. And you do have permission to stay in England from the British government already."

I was stunned. At least a dozen questions ran through my mind, demanding answers.

"But..."

"But nothing. Go to work or you'll get fired. Start walking." Finley pulled me out onto the street and closed the door of the flat behind me.

"We'll discuss it later," he called after me.

I put my left foot in front of the right, like a robot on autopilot, because my mind was engaged elsewhere. What just happened? Did Finley ask me to marry him?

At the factory, I was sloppy, dropping containers on the floor and, several times, my coworkers had to fill in for where I left a hole on the conveyor belt. My hands were shaking and my coworkers' eyebrows were raised. My mind was preoccupied with the events that had happened as quickly as they were unexpected.

How could I not fall in love with the person who lifted such an unsolvable conundrum off my shoulders? My family was safe and I was free. I kept repeating the thought in my mind like a mantra, afraid that it would disappear if I did not hold on tight.

Finley's kindness overwhelmed me. My gratitude grew exponentially and, before I could get a grip on my emotions, Eros pierced my heart and I fell deeply in love. I ran all the way from the pie factory to Finley's flat.

I rang the doorbell. Nothing. *He did say we would talk later?* I rang the bell again. I could hear a shuffle, a curse, and then Finley was standing in the doorway in his pajama bottoms and a t-shirt.

"What the hell are you doing here in the middle of the night?"

"You said we would talk later."

"I meant tomorrow." He was still irritated, but his voice softened.

"I'm so very sorry," I apologized. "I misunderstood. I'm leaving. Please don't be mad. I will wait till tomorrow and we can talk then." I started to leave.

"I'm up now. Come in." Finley pulled me in. "You look out of breath; were you running?"

"No," I lied.

"We might as well talk now. I'll make some tea, but I don't have that voodoo drink you like."

"It's the first time someone called my chamomile tea 'voodoo,'" I said.

"Well, there is a first time for everything," said Finley.

Yes, there is, I thought, but remained silent.

Finley explained that he was helping me out, and in three years, providing both parties agreed, we would be granted a divorce. "A no-contest divorce." He looked at me with questioning eyes. I nodded my head and hastened to offer that I would pay for the divorce.

"Thanks," he said.

We sat at the kitchen table, each with a cup of tea in hand. He was enjoying his, and I tried to read the imaginary leaves floating in mine. To me, divorce seemed far away from this moment of relief and happiness. First, there had to be a marriage, and I would be the best wife Finley could ever imagine. My heart was spinning out of control. Fortunately, my mouth stayed silent. I studied Finley's face for signs of regret. I could not see any.

He put on his favorite Bob Dylan LP.

> *"Close your eyes,*
> *close your door,*
> *you don't have to worry any more,*
> *I'll be your baby tonight..."*

"You heard the man," Finley whispered in my ear.

I closed my eyes.

The next morning, I tore up the letter to my parents. Finley went to work, and I booked the registrar's office for a wedding ceremony on Saturday, December 23rd. It was the soonest date available. That morning, a friend of ours who was going to be the witness met us at the registry office. There was roadwork outside the window, and I had to be prompted to answer the crucial question, because I could not hear the official.

Finley and I walked back. It was sunny and not very cold. The walk seemed to dissipate the awkwardness we felt and soon we hit the old rhythms of our relationship. By the time we reached my flat, it felt like the old times again.

I said, "Christmas Eve tomorrow. Our first Christmas."

"Listen," Finley said slowly, "we cannot see each other anymore. You do understand, don't you?"

I looked down at my feet. I could hear my heart thundering in my chest. Finley put his finger under my chin and lifted my head, forcing me to look up at him like a naughty child.

"This is not a real marriage. You do know that, right? I do like you and I wanted to help you, but I am not ready for an actual marriage. We can stay in touch and be friends, but not lovers."

"Spend Christmas with me," I pleaded. "You have no family here either."

"I cannot. I helped you get your freedom. You owe me mine."

He kissed me on my forehead, turned, and walked away. I stood motionless, my eyes fixed on the pavement. I could not bear to watch him walk out of my life.

In 2021, *Finley's Gift* was selected by **Living Spring Publishers** for their book of fifteen stories from around the world. Still available on Amazon.

becoming anika pavel

Wishing I had put on warm socks before I went to bed the previous night, I was grateful that at least I did remember to put on a warm sweatshirt. I recalled I had played a lot of records and had drunk two bottles of wine that I was saving to drink with my would-be husband. I could see my breath when I blew on my hands in an attempt to warm them up.

I ran into the living room, which was not much warmer, and put a half-crown coin into the gas meter, which was how in-home heat was delivered in those days. The little fireplace started to hiss warmth into the room. After I stopped shivering, my head started to ache. So this was what a hangover feels like. But I could have been dehydrated. I was sure that the amount of wine I drank did not equal the number of tears I cried.

After the second glass, or it could have been the third, I'd decided that I was going to cry out my pain. Kind of like bloodletting in the old days, and so, assisted by wine, I'd let the tears flow till I felt numb. I was not sure if my strategy worked, but for a while at least, I felt more pain in my head than in my heart.

But now I needed to do something. It was Christmas, after all, and I was in London. I was free, and without any consequence to my family back in Czechoslovakia. So what if my heart was in tatters; it would heal. At the age of twenty, most everything heals.

I decided to write a letter to my parents. It was an exercise in creative writing with the emphasis on "creative." I could not tell them that my marriage was a sham, so I described a fictional Christmas full of Slovak traditions. I described the beautiful Christmas tree I did not have and failed to mention that my husband, who'd saved me and my family from the label "illegal emigrant" by the Communist regime in my homeland, was absent.

The high school writer deep inside me took over and I wrote with a flourish about the perfect prune-mushroom-and-potato soup I made from the recipe my mother sent to me in her latest letter. Then, the Christmas potato salad, which, I admitted, did not taste anywhere near as good as my mother's. But the schnitzel saved the day.

I stopped before claiming to make the poppy seed "pupaky" because I knew taking it that far would have given the game away. Instead, I described how I decorated the table I did not own, and promised my parents that it was to be the first of many Slovak Christmases. I would keep up the tradition, I assured them.

The next promise was to myself. I would light the candles and turn off the lights. Then, taking a handful of walnuts, I would throw them into the corners of the room, saying as I did in my childhood, *"Radujte sa kuty vianoce su tu."* Roughly translated, it means, *Corners be happy that Christmas is here.*

I would, in future, tell my children why we did that. It was a way to save some of the treats from Christmas abundance for the days when the winter provisions were at a low point. To find a stray walnut at the end of winter was a treat.

Surprisingly, the letter made me feel better. Not that I believed what I wrote, but somehow it reaffirmed my hope that one day I would have the Christmas I had just described.

The sound of the telephone stopped any further fiction. Tony, my friend and agent, called to wish us "Merry Christmas." I told him I was alone.

"I'll be there in a tick." I tried to convince him that I was fine, but found myself convincing a dead telephone line. I was barely dressed when the doorbell rang.

I left my self-pity in the flat and ate the best meal I'd had in a long time. I became interested in the lives of my fellow diners and found that one of Tony's friends, an actor named Richard, had just bought a house in Willesden Green and was looking for someone to rent the flat on the second floor.

"Really?" I said and explained I needed the flat fast, to which I received a reply, "Is Boxing Day too soon?" My heart may have been drowning in darkness, yet materializing out of nowhere came a ray of sunshine.

"I'll take it," I said, and we shook on it.

I started to hatch a plan in my head. Despite having won a modeling competition, I knew that adventure would have to wait for the time being. I needed a steady income.

Cautiously, I took a sip of the wine that I did not dare to touch through the dinner. My head did not explode, so I took another sip and continued the planning. For the first time in a very long while, I felt I was in control of my future. Thinking of my on-paper husband, I felt a stab in my heart, but I smiled at Richard, the actor who offered me the flat.

The rest of the night was spent in pleasant conversation. In the background, Simon and Garfunkel sang "Bridge over Troubled Water." I made up my mind not to squander the bridge that was just laid over my troubled waters.

At the end of the night, Tony took me back to my flat. I thanked him and apologized for being such a wet rag earlier on.

"So, now that you are staying, you need to do something about your name."

"My name?"

"You cannot be a model with that complicated name of yours; nobody would book you." He paused and then asked, "You aren't thinking of using your married name, are you?"

"No, definitely not," I said.

"Okay, let's change your last name first," said Tony. "Something foreign but pronounceable."

"How about Pavel?" I asked. My brother's name was Pavel; my uncle's name was Pavel, and nobody in England would know that it was a boy's first name.

"Good, very good," said Tony. "Good start."

"I like it," I said. "Jarmila Pavel."

"No, no, no, we cannot have Jarmila. People would spell it with a Y when they hear it and pronounce it God only knows how when they see it written. What about Anita?"

"How about Anika?" I wanted to keep the name as Slovak as possible.

We agreed, and Anika Pavel was born.

When we arrived at the flat, I thanked Tony and apologized again for being such a wet rag earlier on.

"Get your beauty sleep, my dear, you look like you need it," said Tony. Then he whispered in my ear as we said goodbye, "Whatever you were doing last night, don't do it again." He kissed me on both cheeks. I understood his gentle scolding and promised not to cry. I did not own up to the wine.

"Sleep well, Anika Pavel," he said, and drove off.

"Welcome home, Anika Pavel," I said as I opened the door to the flat. The name felt right and already I owned it. If I were going to forsake my father's name, at least I would keep the family favorite name, Pavel, alive.

Back in the empty bedroom, sleep eluded me. I closed my eyes, but my mind was running toward the future like Don Quixote toward his windmills, ready to fight any obstacles the future might bring me...and I fought...losing some, winning others.

Photograph by Barry Weller

a statement

After more than an hour, the landlord, who was not thrilled to meet me on Boxing Day, finally arrived. I handed the irritated man the flat's keys, pocketed half of my deposit, and turned toward the Underground. I was determined to leave the flat and the Soviet invasion of my homeland behind and focus on my future. In the West. Czechoslovakia was locked in the East and the key was in the Kremlin. And there was nothing I could do about it.

I got off at the Underground station and savored the walk toward my new life. I opened the door to my new abode. A large bay window overlooked the street. Walm Lane. The rectangular table was disproportionately long and narrow. The two chairs tucked under the narrow end of the table gave an impression it was meant for two people who did not like to talk to each other. The sofa was really a single bed with some big cushions leaning against the wall. Other than that, the room was empty. The sparseness inspired me. Like my future, it had possibilities.

I settled in and after welcoming the New Year alone, I took the Tube down to Piccadilly. The early January day was cool but sunny. Just as I turned to Carnaby Street, in the window of one of the fashionable boutiques, I noticed a sign: "Cashier Needed."

England had not converted to the metric system yet, so there were twenty shillings in a pound and twelve pence in a shilling. Not to mention twenty-one shillings in a guinea. The carryover was complicated, and math was not my biggest strength. But I was taught to never give up without a try. I applied for the job.

The manager and his assistant suggested that I was too pretty to be a cashier and perhaps I could do some modeling for them. I could hear the warning bells ringing in my ears. I told them I wanted the cashier job. They tried one more time to convince me, so I asked, "Do you need a cashier or not?" They did, and I got the job.

After I worked at the shop for a while, I learned the two men's pattern. When a pretty young girl came into the shop, they would engage her in conversation, flatter her, and then offer her a job modeling for the shop. The boutique was famous and known to be frequented by stars. In a place where both the employees' and the customers' average age was early twenties, the manager, who was in his fifties, seemed trustworthy. It was always he who suggested to talk it over in his office. I did not know how they convinced the girls to take the "test shots," but they did. Most of them, anyway.

The two voyeurs had empty cameras set up, and the girls had to change their clothes right there in front of them. They would get the girls to do all sorts of poses no real photographer would ask a fashion model to do. I would hear all the details after the girl left. The two sleazy men would brag about their exploits to the salesman in the shop. They thought my English was not good enough to understand what was going on, or they just did not care.

One unusually warm day in early March, the assistant manager was dressed for summer. I busied myself with filing receipts and invoices. He tried to get my attention, and I did my best to ignore him. Finally, he stood right in front of the register where I could see his whole body.

"What do you think of my new trousers?" he said. They were light blue, as tight as they possibly could be, and it was clear he was not wearing underwear.

"I bet you would like to get some of this." He stared at me, stroking his thigh.

I turned to the manager and gave him my one-week notice. But the two leeches were determined to get me undressed. A few days later we received a shipment of shirts. Toward the end of the day, the manager asked me to try on one of the shirts.

"Apparently," he told me, "several customers complained about the fitting." Despite the fact that I had seen it all before, foolishly, I thought he would not try it on me.

"All right," I said, and walked toward the dressing room.

"No, we need to make notes. Come to the manager's office," said the assistant manager.

I looked around and realized the shop was empty. All the salespeople had gone home. With supreme effort, I controlled my shaking hands, put the shirt on the counter, picked up my handbag from the chair next to the cash register, and walked to the entrance door. I was convinced they could hear the sound of my heart thundering in my chest. The key was in the lock and

I managed to turn it. With my way to safety secure, a rush of fury came over me and I turned around and showed them my middle finger.

Not quite a "Me Too" moment, but in the late-sixties London, a statement.

the velvet car

The day started innocuously enough. Two auditions for modeling jobs in the morning and a three-hour fashion shoot in the afternoon, after which I headed to a restaurant for my evening shift. I held on to the waitressing job because I needed steady income to send medical supplies to my mother in Czechoslovakia, who was still fighting cancer, and the "wonderful" Communist health system did not have the medicine she needed. After a rather boring night at the restaurant, I was looking forward to my bed.

Sitting in a mostly empty Underground car, I slipped off my shoes for the duration of the train ride. Waitressing took a toll on the feet of someone even as young as twenty-three years old. I got off the train and noticed a car idling in front of the station and a man at the steering wheel. I felt mildly jealous that some person, after a day's work, would get a ride home and I had to walk.

I started my walk down the tree-lined street, so pleasant during the day, but in the middle of the night I always felt uncomfortable. I was aware of the sound of my footsteps when suddenly I realized the car, still without a passenger, was following me. There was nobody else on the street, just the car and me. If I sped up, the car sped up. It was as if the driver was playing a game. I could hear my heart racing at the speed I wished my legs could match.

I ran my fingers over the two keys inside my coat pocket and decided which one was for the front door of the house. I prayed I was right. As long as he stayed behind me, I had a chance.

The car slowed down as if for the person to get out. I took off and ran. With the key in my outstretched hand, I managed to put the key straight into the keyhole, turned it, opened the door while pulling the key out and, thankfully, the door locked automatically behind me. I never switched on the lights. I ran up the stairs in darkness. I unlocked and then locked my flat door.

With my back leaning on the door, I slid down to the floor. I held my hands over my heart. My whole body started to shake. I sat on my hands, hoping to steady at least some part of me. I felt thirsty but did not dare to move. I listened for the sound of footsteps. Then I heard soft knocking on the flat's big bay window. I froze, and then…nothing.

When I came to, I realized that I had passed out. Luckily for me, I was already on the floor. I also noticed that it was raining. It was the rain I had heard tapping on the window, but I was unable to move from the floor. As I watched the sun come up, I made the decision to get a roommate and a car.

With Rosemary I gained not only a roommate, I gained a whole new group of friends. Soon Catherine, Rosemary's friend from high school, moved in with us. With the money I saved from the rent, it was not long before I could start looking for a car.

The only car I could afford was a velvet-green Ford Anglia. It actually had a velvet exterior. The car's sticker price was 187 pounds. I had 200 pounds. I bought the car and paid with cash in small bills.

The salesman was not amused and told me I should have gone to a bank to convert the small bills to "proper money." The scolding went over my head because I was focused on the fact that I had just bought a car! I knew that no person my age at home, in Communist Czechoslovakia, could possibly buy a car and that made me very proud.

The car was probably worth much more, if not for the green velvet outside. Apparently, even in psychedelic-era London, a velvet car was not an easy sell. I was the benefactor. It had never occurred to me that I might want to sell it someday. Where I came from, if you were lucky enough to buy a car, you kept it for life.

After I paid the mandatory insurance, and the road tax, I had no money left for driving school. Rosemary's friend Geoffrey drove me to a large, unused parking lot. He spent two hours teaching me how to drive. I got the driving part pretty fast, but shifting the gears was giving me problems. Undeterred, I felt sure I would get better with practice.

I parked the car right in front of the house where I lived. I looked out the windows often so that I could see my green-velvet car to reassure myself that I owned a car.

Every day I allocated one hour to practice driving the car. But learning how to change gears without ruining my transmission proved to be a challenge. I did put a big red plastic L on the front and back of my car, as was required, and I bought a learner's permit. I practiced the three-point turn until I could do it with my eyes closed. (Not that I ever did).

At the beginning, it was frustrating. The road sloped slightly on each side toward the curb, and it was hard to get the clutch and the gas just right, so I would not start rolling backward. Luckily, the car did not pick up much speed before it hit the curb. I banged my fist on the dashboard many times in tears of fury, wishing I could give up. But I owned the darn thing; I had to learn how to drive it.

Eventually I mastered the beast and felt confident to drive the car all around London as long as I had someone in the passenger seat. It was not legal for a learner to drive alone. The fact that most of the time the person sitting next to me had no driver's license, in fact could not drive at all, missed my consciousness.

Having to stop and start on the hill still made me nervous. Hitting the balance between easing off the clutch with one foot and pressing the other foot on the gas just the right amount often proved tricky, and I would start rolling backward for just a moment, but long enough to speed up my heartbeat.

The first time I took the driving test, I failed. But I was ready for it. Apparently, no *girl* at the time had passed the test the first time she took it. Or so my tester-gentleman told me with glee, before I even started my routine of three-point turn, etc. So, with that dubious evidence, when I passed the test on the second try, I considered it to be de facto first.

With my still-warm driver's license in hand, I took Saturday off from work and invited my friends to go out with me in my car. For a girl from a Communist country, drinking Coca-Cola was equivalent to having a "drink," so I was the perfect designated driver.

We decided to go north of Watford, which to Londoners amounted to going to the country. There was a pub whose owner Geoffrey knew, and he assured us we would get at least one free drink.

On the way back, Rosemary, who was sitting in the front with me, pointed out with some curiosity that there was smoke coming out of the bonnet (hood) of my car. I pondered what to do for just a moment longer when flames started to come out. Everybody in the car screamed and Geoffrey yelled, "Pull over and get out of the car."

He took off his shirt and kept beating it on the fire until he extinguished it. We all stood around the car like lost ducks until a good Samaritan pulled over and took us to the nearest Tube station. After that, Geoffrey showed me how to check my oil and water and told me to do it each time I bought petrol for my car.

Many years later, the ability to drive stick made me the coolest mum in our neighborhood.

frank zappa

The Communist regime in Czechoslovakia granted women married to a foreign national legal emigrant status, according to which I was allowed to live abroad legally. I always found it hypocritical that the same privilege was not granted to men. The country that beat its chest about being emancipated expected the woman to follow her husband, but not the other way around.

However, I was not going to complain, because the further perk was that a member of my family was allowed to visit me, but only one at a time. Everyone still had to get an exit visa first from the local government office before they could ask for an entry visa from the British Embassy in Prague, but the bottom line was, a member of my family would be most likely granted permission to visit me.

One would think that, since both my parents were pensioners, the government would recognize the financial benefit to the country should my parents emigrate and forfeit their pension. But controlling people was far more important to the Communist regime than the economy. Furthermore, the official who granted the exit visa would be in trouble with the Communist Party if the recipient of the exit visa did not return. I realize that the whole concept of exit visa would be completely foreign to US citizens, but such was the state of affairs for us in Communist Czechoslovakia.

Ultimately, it was about fear and self-preservation. Once the hurdle of the exit visa was conquered, my mother vowed not to let some pesky cancer stop her from seeing her daughter.

Easter in England can be cold and rainy, but that was not the case the year my mother came to visit me. We took full advantage of the exceptional weather. Sitting on top of the double-decker bus, I took my mother to all my favorite sights. We banished any thoughts of cancer and enjoyed her remission. I wanted to treat my mother to one meal in a restaurant, and she insisted she would pick the place. I knew that she would not want me to spend too much money on her and would not enjoy an expensive meal.

After wandering around the West End for a while, she settled on a place, the name of which I no longer remember, only that it was near the Palladium. There was nothing memorable about the restaurant except the gusto with which my mother ate her food. For dessert, she ordered pancakes with strawberries and whipped cream. At first, I felt disappointed that she would not order something more English, something she never ate before. But when I saw her enjoying the dish, which I remember her cooking for me many times in my childhood, I started to laugh. I took a taste and although good, the pancakes were nowhere near as good as I remembered hers to be.

"There is a secret ingredient in these pancakes," she assured me. "I did not have to make them."

My mother reminisced about how my brothers and I, and often several of our friends, would be standing in line next to the stove, and as soon as she would take the pancake off the pan, it would disappear onto one of the waiting plates. This would go on often for hours.

"By the time you all finished eating and I could sit down with a few leftover pancakes, they tasted like *hovno* (shit)."

I remembered the image my mother was describing well. I felt belated guilt for so freely inviting my friends to come over and have pancakes at my house. But what shocked me was my mother using the "S" word. I had never heard her say it before. My mother never used even dubious words. Seeing my perplexed face, she started to laugh.

"You think that I cannot say the word?"

I felt a shift in our relationship. She did not need to be the authority figure anymore. She had taught me all I needed to know. More importantly, I realized, she believed I learned all that she had taught me, which allowed her to lighten up. For me to find I had a friend who I knew would never let me down was an insurance that could not be bought.

We were heading toward Piccadilly Circus and on our way, we found almost everything funny. My mother found some of the sixties' fashion particularly hilarious.

Piccadilly had a special meaning for me. I often sat at the Shaftesbury fountain just watching people. It was my *bridge over troubled water*, my source of strength from which I drew often. I was glad to put in some happy memories for the future. Being there with my mother in her newly defined role as a friend was going to be gold in the bank.

In a shop window selling British memorabilia to the tourists, my mother spotted a poster of Frank Zappa sitting on the toilet with his pants loitering at his feet. Given that we were in a kind of toilet humor mood already, this was too much for my mother. She started to laugh so hard that I joined her, before knowing what set her off, thinking that laughter was indeed contagious. Unable to get a coherent word out, she kept gesticulating and pointing at Frank Zappa. To onlookers our behavior must have looked like a bizarre game of charades. Finally, I figured out that she too needed a toilet.

The closest bathrooms I knew about were the public bathrooms at the beginning of Carnaby Street. I steered her toward our target, which was quite a way away.

"Don't laugh," I said seriously, and my stern voice seemed to have reversed our roles.

"I must not laugh," my mother repeated like a naughty girl and promptly burst out laughing.

We both knew that her last surgery made continence a challenge. I prayed for divine help to allow us to reach the public bathrooms before it was too late.

"We made it," I announced as I guided my mother down the stairs and into the open stall. I closed the door behind her and breathed a sigh of relief.

"Not really," came the report from inside the stall.

I knew all the shops were closed so I was glad that my mother wore her skirt length substantially below her knees, but I would not dare to suggest that she go commando.

"If Frank Zappa can drop his pants," she said, coming out of the toilet and walking to the garbage bin, where, with dramatic gesture, she dropped her underwear and said, "so can I."

time to say goodbye

My best friend and roommate, Rosemary, married her boyfriend, Barry, and they moved to Australia. At the grand old age of twenty-three, I found myself alone and once again floating in uncertainty. I missed my friends. My mother's visit provided a delay in the decisions I knew I would have to face and soon. With my family's needs eased into the background, I found myself on life's stage with the spotlight on me.

I saw myself on the pages of fashion magazines and on commercials, both in movie theaters and on television. I had a little break into television working with Frankie Howard on his show *Oh, You Are Awful*. I appeared in a movie with Dick Emery, which to my mother's delight was seen back home.

But the dust-covered little girl who always hung around the local boy group with her brothers had a hard time believing her success. Especially pertaining to her looks.

My physical insecurity notwithstanding, I had a more important ambition I had to revisit first.

Looking at the empty page of a wire-bound notebook was exhilarating. I gave up on writing once before when I first learned English because English words would interfere in my Slovak thoughts. Surely now I could separate the two languages. I would have preferred to write in English because by now I thought in English. However, because I learned English mainly from listening, my spelling left too much to be desired and so I decided to write in Slovak.

I picked up one of the pens on my kitchen table and started to write. I had no typewriter and computers did not exist, so I wrote by hand. I wrote the rest of that day and all night, eating only cashew nuts and water.

The story was based in Prague and in London. The hero was a young man who discovers that his father was a gestapo chief responsible for the killing of the whole village where his mother was from, whom he raped and impregnated.

"The bastard will always remind you of me," were his last words as he set her free.

Soon the English started to insert itself into the flow of my thinking, especially in dialog, so I convinced myself that it was okay to use English in dialog. It would help me, I told myself, to keep up with the speed with which my imagination was running.

I kept on writing until I saw the sun coming up. I went to bed and fell into deep, satisfying sleep. When I woke up the sun was on its way down again.

With a cup of coffee in one hand and hard-boiled egg in the other, hungrily I started to read the labor of the night before. The line between my eyes became deeper with each page. After

Reunion in NYC after 40 years – Catherine, Rosemary and I

I finished reading what I'd hoped would be the beginning of a gripping story, I threw the notebook in the garbage and paced the floor. The writing was a mix of English and Slovak, without any notion which language would show up in the next sentence, resulting in gibberish that even I had a hard time following. The story, I still felt, was gripping, but only as long as it stayed in my head. I was unable to translate it to either language.

I sat on the floor surrounded by my notes and torn pages from the night before. Reluctantly, I bid farewell to my writing ambition. With the drama I thought was proportionate to my disappointment, I slept on the floor wrapped in my mother's comfort sweater.

Next morning, I put my writing ambition on an unreachable shelf and moved on to my next pressing problem I had to solve. My living situation.

With my friends gone to the Land Down Under, I had no appetite to look for new roommates. Ignoring my intuition, I decided to move in with my boyfriend. It was the seventies and nobody raised an eyebrow. I knew he was not a friend with a capital S as in Stand by Me, but I told myself it was temporary.

But before I could truly move on, I had to fulfil an important obligation.

* * *

The red beret sat on my head like a question mark. I tilted my head to one side and the beret looked approvingly at me in the mirror; I moved it further toward my left ear and walked outside.

I had an appointment at Her Majesty's court. Every day I was aware of the benefits of my marriage, the memory of which was no longer painful. I was one of those political brides who was foolish enough to fall in love with the man who was simply helping her out. To my surprise, the divorce proved to be less painful than the wedding. I submitted the paperwork, paid the fee, and with a gavel of the judge, I was a young divorcee.

I walked out of the court to the street physically and legally alone and wandered the streets of London in typical English weather. It appeared to be raining, but one did not get wet. I thought it was symbolic of my situation. I was in limbo, neither here nor there.

I bought the *Variety* newspaper from time to time to look for auditions and to see what shows or movies were being made in London. On the third page I saw an advertisement for the Playboy Club. I had seen it before but never actually read the advertisement. This time, I read on. I realized working at the

Playboy Club would help me save a lot of money. The flexible hours and time off for any film work were the main attraction for showbiz folk who worked there. Of course, the above-average pay didn't hurt. It was tempting. After all, it was just waitressing in an uncomfortable costume and ridiculously high heels.

I was not worried about the ogling men; I met plenty of them in the restaurant, not to mention in the modeling world. The fact was that a girl could encounter sleazy people anywhere, and the difference in wages was undeniable. Still, I hesitated. The Communist propaganda with its unlikely partner, women's lib, gave me a reason to pause.

I kept my evening job as a waitress in a small restaurant on Wigmore Street, not trusting the lying eye of the camera. Modeling, however, continued to go well and I became a regular on *The Two Ronnies* show at the BBC. Nothing big, background really, but it was something to put on my resume. I checked *Variety* for acting lessons.

One day after lunch during the rehearsals at the BBC, I lingered in the cafeteria to finish a letter to my mother. I was surprised when the producer of the show stopped by me and asked what I was doing. I told him I was writing to my mother.

"You know, you should take elocution lessons. We could use you in some of the sketches, but we cannot understand you."

I was confused. "But I never had a speaking part."

"I know, but we can hear you in the control room talking to people on set, and you are hard to understand."

I said "thank you" and promised to think about it.

Later on, Terry Hughes, the producer of *The Two Ronnies* who gave me that advice, went to America to direct *The Golden Girls* and I never saw him again. But I did take his advice.

I looked through *Variety* again, to find elocution classes. The price told me I could not afford them. I reread the *Playboy* advertisement. Simple math told me that with the salary *Playboy* offered, I could pay for both my acting classes and my elocution classes and have a guaranteed income.

I called the Playboy Club and was told to come for an audition on the following Saturday. "All right," I thought, "I can do audition, I have done that plenty of times."

I walked to the club feeling foolish and excited in equal measures. I spotted two girls I was sure I saw on a modeling audition. I was not sure if that was good or bad, but before I could decide, it was my turn to be interviewed. I was hired right away. No "we'll let your agent know..." They knew right away that they wanted me for the job. I remember I had a very positive feeling walking out of the building on Park Lane. For the first time in a very long time, I knew how much money I was going to get at the end of the week. I could calculate with certainty what I could afford and I could plan ahead. Despite the rain, it was a very sunny day for me. Best of all, no wait. I was told I would be starting a three-week training program on Monday.

the playboy club

"Put your cuties in," said the diminutive seamstress with an infectious smile.

The seamstress room where all the girls were fitted for their bunny costumes was on the fifth floor of the Playboy Club. I finished my training, during which time I had to wear the "retired" costumes left behind by the girls who left the club. The costumes were in too good a condition to be discarded and so were used for the bunnies in training. Not all girls who went through the three-week training program made it onto the floor.

"What could possibly take them three weeks to teach me?" I rolled my eyes none too discreetly when I first heard it would take three weeks before I could be a fully trained bunny. "I've waited tables before," I thought. Boy, was I in for a surprise.

While Europe seldom used ice in the drinks and beer was drunk warmish, I soon learned that in America, serving a drink without ice cubes was unthinkable. The restaurants where I worked were small and run by owner or staff who knew little more than I did.

The Playboy Club was a vast organization run with a high degree of professionalism, which was expected from all the employees. Because it was members only, the level of customer service expected was high and was heavily tilted toward satisfying the American customer. All drinks, with an exception of beer, were served in glasses full of ice.

There was cube ice and there was crushed ice and the beer glass had to be chilled. The bunny had to use the right glass, right ice, and right garnish for each drink and have it on her tray in the right order. Meaning in the same way the bottles were standing in the bar. Scotch, gin, vodka, rum...etc. Make a mistake and the bartender would roar. How much of a roar depended on how busy a night it was and what mood the bartender was in. The bunny did her own bills and added them up, although the room director had to sign off on them. If her math was faulty too often, she could face dismissal.

I soon learned that this level of professionalism was expected in every detail and nothing was forgotten, from the moment the bunny introduced herself to the moment she handed in the bill to the bartender, who would ring it up. At the end of the night, the bunny had to add up all her bills and they had to match the bartender's cash register. These were the little-known duties of the bunny girls.

After Ursula Andress raised from the water in her bikini in the James Bond Dr. No movie, bikini-clad girls filled the beaches of Europe and America. Yet, the bunny costume was attacked relentlessly. Ironically, the costume was based on the corset worn by women in the nineteenth century, complete with whale bone in the bodice, which was shipped from the US. The rest would be fitted on the girl by the seamstress in each location.

The future began to emerge, and I liked it. The modeling work was going well and despite the grueling work in high heels at night, I felt happy. For me, The Playboy Club became the place where I saw familiar faces every time I came to work. I was not just a face in a magazine that would be gone when the next issue came out.

When my relationship with my boyfriend deteriorated, I moved in with bunny Tricia and her sister Carmel. I was thankful for the way they welcomed me. Having grown up with two brothers, I was learning what it was like to have sisters.

When the ex-boyfriend came into the club and threatened me, the playboy employees stood by me.

"If anything happened to your face, you are finished," he breathed into my ear. "You are nothing without your face."

The night manager got one of the security guys on duty to drive behind my car all the way to the flat I was sharing with Carmel and Tricia. He waited till I was safely inside before I saw the lights of his car make a U-turn and drive back toward the Club.

Carmel's flat in Fulham had two bedrooms. One larger where Carmel slept, and the smaller one was Tricia's. When the sisters offered for me to stay, Tricia moved in with Carmel and I had Tricia's bedroom to myself, and this free of charge!

I decided that I never, ever wanted to find myself on the street with my two suitcases again, in order to secure personal freedom from an ex-boyfriend. I opened a savings account at the Building Society (a type of British banking institution similar to a credit union). I put every pound I could save into that account and soon I started to see pleasant results. My savings grew exponentially thanks in no small way to Carmel and Tricia's generosity.

In the VIP room

For a while, I could indulge in being young and having fun. Playboy attracted a lot of celebrities and on weekends I allowed myself to go to nightclubs and have fun and dance the night away. I remember a hilarious evening when Tricia did a Peter Sellers Pink Panther impersonation—to Peter Sellers, who to his credit found it funny, but then, it was four a.m.

Alas, the waters under my bridge were once more troubled. My mother had a relapse. Her cancer came back with a vengeance. She had undergone a colostomy and I went home to help my father cope. The doctors gave my mother minimal hope for survival. But they did not know my mother. She fought a valiant battle and, after two months, I went back to England believing she won. If not the war, she had at least won the battle.

It was at that time that I fully realized how fortunate I was that Playboy let me take any length of time off, but more importantly, let me come back to work and have an immediate income. I needed to supply the adhesive bags for my mother's colostomy, because they did not have them in Czechoslovakia. The doctor also asked me to supply B12 injections and a few other medical necessities to make her comfortable and to build up her health. I arranged for automatic shipments, which also meant that before I could contemplate buying myself a sandwich, I had to make sure there was enough money in my account to cover the expenses for the supplies my mother had to have.

The modeling work picked up too, which helped me reach my goal to buy my own flat. I bought a one-bedroom flat in Ealing. My parents were delighted and proud. Mum insisted that she was well enough for my father to go to London and help me. My brother Pavel was married by then and lived with my parents, so my mother was not going to be alone.

Dad made me curtains, lay down the carpet, and after a friend gave me an old sofa and chair, my father made the new covers, which made the sofa look brand new. Together we painted the place and we wallpapered my bedroom door as well with pink flower by Laura Ashley. By the time my father left, as far as I was concerned, The Hilton Hotel could not compete with my "palace."

To celebrate the successful transformation of my first home, I took my father to the Playboy Club for dinner. I had to get special permission from the bunny mother, which was not hard to do. Bringing a parent to the club was within the rules. I booked the VIP room. According to my mother, Dad would tell everyone who would listen about his dinner at the VIP room at the London Playboy Club. The girls who worked that night knew it was not easy to get out from Communist Czechoslovakia and they treated him like a celebrity. We took pictures for my father and to give Brezhnev's crew something to chew on.

I had no doubt that there were aspects of the Playboy culture that would scandalize people far more liberal than Mary Whitehouse, but I already knew that a girl did not have to wear a bunny costume to be sexually harassed.

Mary Whitehouse was the socially conservative Member of Parliament who fought against the liberal media, the sexual revolution, feminism, and gay rights. She could not have asked for a better symbol for her fight against a permissive society than the London Playboy Club. She was determined to close the club down and it was because of that constant threat, the rules of No smoking, no drinking, no dating customers, were strictly enforced. But for me the dinner with my father at the VIP room will forever demonstrate that if you want, you can find goodness in the most unexpected place.

the roller-coaster

My parents and my brother were involved in a car accident. It was not very serious, but I flew home anyway. During that time my modeling agency split in two. Or so I was told. Because I was not there, I was moved to the Soho office.

The uneven supply of work in the world of modeling and acting was par for the course. You could have triple booking one day and have to say no to two of them, followed by complete silence for the next few weeks. At first, I did not think much of it. The fact that I could just up my work at the Playboy Club made me blind to the situation a lot longer than I should have been. What opened my eyes was not so much the infrequency of the work as the quality of the work.

The first time the audition made me uncomfortable was with an American director. The girl who opened the door to his apartment left shortly after I sat down. The man looked through my portfolio, then proceeded to tell me that he was once engaged to Ava Gardner and I reminded him of her. He said he would like to see me again and would call the agent.

I got out as fast as I could and told my agent I did not want to see him again. "He was creepy," I told her.

My next job was with a female photographer whose studio was deep in London's East End in a very shaky neighborhood. I was asked to bring lots of changes but only tops and hats. It was an hour booking and I spent as long to travel there and even longer back since I hit rush hour. The photographer took only headshots with me doing my hair and makeup myself. She picked what she wanted me to wear. She worked really fast and was able to complete five headshots. Later I saw my face on the covers of some second-grade magazines for which I knew she got paid a lot more than I did.

"You don't want to get a reputation of being a brat," said my agent when I complained.

"Next time, one session, one cover. And a minimum two-hour booking," I said.

My next audition was to meet with another movie producer who was working for a big US company. I was to meet him at the Dorchester Hotel. Not totally unheard of for an audition to be held in the hotel, but usually there would be several people with clipboards at the door and it would be one room for the casting and one for models/actresses to wait in.

I walked straight into a dimly lit hotel room. The man in his sixties was lying on the bed in his dressing gown.

"Sit down and tell me about yourself," he said.

I started to tell him about my credits when he interrupted me. "No, tell me about you. I am interested in you."

I got out of the room as fast as I could, called the agent, and told her I just left the agency. I am not sure what took me so long to leave. Loyalty, I suppose. I did get a lot of work through her before the agency split.

That night at the Playboy Club I worked with a bunny I knew was quite a successful model. She told me about a new, vibrant agency called Freddie's. I had heard of them before, but I also heard through gossip that Freddie once dated Finley. I hesitated, but I needed an agent urgently and I figured if she hired me, I could be sure I was dealing with a sophisticated woman whom I would like to work with.

I made an appointment and got hired.

The quality of my work improved exponentially. Soon I was auditioning for Sam Peckinpah, a real American director who interviewed me in an office with a client and four other people present. They sat on one side of the table while I sat across while they all looked at my book.

The commercial was for a Japanese clothing company and the star was James Coburn, whom I remember as kind and surprisingly funny.

I was told to see Mr. Peckinpah during our lunch break. He invited me to sit next to him. Because of my own background, it would not be the first nor last time that people in showbiz would ask me if I knew Milos Forman. I had my standard reply ready: I knew of him and I had seen his movies, both the Czech and in English, but no, I did not know him personally. A longwinded reply to make sure I covered all potential questions.

Sam Peckinpah asked about the political situation in Czechoslovakia and of course, when and how I got out.

"Interesting story," he said. "I am interested to hear more.

Call me at the studio and we'll talk some more." He looked at his watch. "Now it's time to go back to work."

Next day I had an early call at The Pinewood Studios to shoot my scene for *The Spy Who Loved Me* with Roger Moore. A big week for me. The roles were small, but the productions were significant.

By the time I called the telephone number Sam Peckinpah gave me, it was the end of the week. I was put on hold several times then was told Mr. Peckinpah had left. I tried again on Monday and again on Tuesday. By the time I got through to Sam Peckinpah, he was leaving for the US. He told me to contact him the next time I was in California, which of course I did not. Once again, I told myself, "He would not remember me." I always feared to come across as too self-important.

Perhaps for the same reason I never list all the movies I have had a small part in as many of them ended on the cutting room floor. However, I did meet some very interesting people on the set. Glenda Jackson, with whom I had an interesting political discussion on the set of the movie *The Class of Miss MacMichael*, and the aforementioned Sam Peckinpah spring to mind. I was not at all surprised when Miss Jackson went into politics.

Then there was Roger Moore, with whom I did another movie far less visible, for me, not for him. Roger Moore I always found to be a gentleman and who to my surprise remembered me when I met him in NYC many years later.

I auditioned for *The Golden Lady* with half of London and somehow landed one of the starring parts.

On a mission to Egypt, James Bond 007 (ROGER MOORE) finds himself surrounded by Arabian beauties played by, left to right, DAWN RODRIGUES and ANIKA PAVEL, and sitting, JILL GOODALL and FELICITY YORK in "The Spy Who Loved Me," released by United Artists, a Transamerica Company.

the unlikely friends

For the time being, my mother had the upper hand over her cancer and so she insisted my father go and visit me in England. She would be fine by herself. It was important to prove to herself that she could take care of herself.

I was busy promoting the James Bond movie and I hoped my father would get the chance to see me in the papers. At the same time, I lost the part of the Russian partisan Maritza in the movie *Force 10 from Navarone*, to Barbara Bach, who was the female star of the James Bond movie we were both in. Both roles were to play a Russian.

Feeling dejected, I blamed the Russians, or, as they insisted being called, Soviets. My disappointment needed an outlet and so on our way from the airport, I vented to my father about the Russian curse. My father, who had been known to blame the Russians for bad weather, noted that he arrived on an airplane, a journey I was able to pay for, and we were driving in my own car to an apartment I owned. I got his subtle message to stop complaining.

"You know what your grandmother Katarina would say." He looked at me as I kept my eyes on the road.

"God helps those who help themselves." I hid my smile. Whenever there was a mention of God, Dad would defer the credit to Grandmother Katarina.

Walking into my flat, my father noticed the poster of Dubcek I had framed and hung on the wall.

"You would not be able to have that back home," he observed.

"I know." I got his subtle hint. "Let's go out and have fish and chips," I said, knowing it was my father's favorite.

* * *

Comedian Benny Hill's show was extremely popular, so when my agent told me she had scheduled a reading for Benny Hill, I was delighted. I wrote down the address and drove at the appointed time for my reading. I took my father with me, explaining he would not be able to come with me but I knew he would be happy to walk up and down looking at the beautiful houses in South Kensington.

I rang the bell and Benny himself opened the door. I brought my book, but he waved it away. "I know what you look like," he said, handing me the script. He laid out the sketch for me and we went over each line slowly. Benny could tell I was nervous, and he did his best to boost my confidence.

The first read did not go well, but Benny just smiled and we read the script again. It was called *The Police Raid in Waterloo Station*. After the third read, which went much better, Benny said, "Let's take a break." He knew I was from Czechoslovakia and he wanted to know how I got to be in England, being aware that travel from Communist countries was not allowed. While we talked, he made me a cup of tea. I mentioned that my father was visiting me, and he was downstairs waiting for me.

"Why did you not bring him up with you?" Benny was genuinely shocked. "Go down and fetch him."

I went to get my father, who as it happened was walking toward me. My father was pleased but worried that he might be a burden.

"He wouldn't have invited you unless he meant it," I reassured my father.

My dad spoke to everyone who did not speak Slovak in German. To my surprise, Benny answered in German.

There I sat on the sofa sipping tea made by Benny Hill and watched my father completely relaxed, communicating with one of the biggest comedy stars of the time.

I will never know if my father's presence had influenced Benny's decision, but I did get the part of Midnight in the sketch.

The Raid on the Waterloo Station

leap year

I could not believe my luck when I got a job for a three-week modeling trip to Singapore, Hong Kong, and Tokyo. It was sponsored by the British government to promote British textiles. Twelve designers were represented, so there was quite a group of us. I am embarrassed to say I no longer remember the designer whose work I was modeling, but I do have a few pictures of the garments, with me in them, naturally. My mother was ecstatic for me and I responded by sending her many postcards from each place I visited. It was faster than waiting for the pictures to be developed, which, eventually I did as well. I fell in love with Hong Kong. I could not have known it was a precursor of time to come. Our last night in Japan we were in Osaka and a big spread was laid out for us. I loved Japanese food and ate myself silly. The journey back was long to start with, but our layover in Alaska took much longer than it was scheduled, so by the time I got back to my flat, I fell into a deep sleep.

I am not sure how long the phone had been ringing when I picked it up. I held the telephone in my hand, still half asleep, trying to listen to my friend Jana.

"You have to come to my birthday and meet him."

"Who?" I asked.

"I found you a husband," she said, apparently for the second time.

I forced myself to open the other eye.

"This is a leap year, and you know I celebrate my birthday only on my actual birthday, February Twenty-Ninth."

"Every four years," I finished for her.

"When did you get back?" she asked.

"About four hours ago," I said.

"Oh, sorry to wake you. Go back to sleep and I'll fill you in later." She hung up. I thought that she could have started with that question, and I would have been back sleeping by now.

I had just returned from a three-week modeling trip to Singapore, Hong Kong, and Japan and so I faced the dilemma of whether to go back to sleep and get much-needed rest but stay on Tokyo time, or should I get up and force myself to join London time? I allowed myself one stretch and then called my friend back.

"I found you a husband." She repeated her earlier statement.

She had done this before. Introduced me to a man she thought was perfect for me and who turned out to be, well, let's just say, less than perfect.

"I can find my own boyfriend. Thanks, but no thanks."

"Husband," Jana corrected me, "this is husband material."

"If you say so." I got the details for the party and said goodbye.

No use arguing. I had to go to her birthday party, and I had to meet this, whoever, and then tell her again, "Take your yenta nose out of my life."

Jana and I met at the Playboy Club. She too was a bunny and we were both from Czechoslovakia but we seldom discussed the situation at home. We did, however, talk to each other in our native language. She spoke Czech and I spoke Slovak, but we were both bilingual and we hardly noticed the difference.

Our relationship, however, was anchored in the present. Jana had married an American businessman, and she wanted the same for me. We were good friends, yet very different. She wanted a husband and I needed a partner.

The day of Jana's birthday, we met at her office. She explained that the man I was about to meet was her husband's company lawyer, and was away on business but would arrive in time for her party.

I was irrationally angry with a man I had never met for being late to the party I was scheming to leave as soon as possible.

When he arrived, I met a tall, slim, young man with a mustache and light, curly hair. Well, this would not work, I told myself. I could never date anybody with a mustache. He said "Hi," and Good God, he was an American!

Really? No mustache and no American? When did that decision come about?

Even my subconscious knew I was phony. Something about this man threatened to destabilize me. My defense mechanisms shifted into high gear. Our interaction that night was unpleasant, to say the least. Jim, he told me was his name, deflected my attacks very well, which made me angry. Jana pulled me into the loo.

"Why are you acting as if you had a hornet's nest in your ass?"

I realized my behavior was absurd. To save some dignity, I left early under the pretense of an early morning call. Jana made a point of calling me extra early.

"I wanted to catch you before you leave," she said smugly, knowing I had no early call. "So what did you think of Jim?" she asked casually.

After spending the night beating myself up for my unreasonable behavior, I was glad that she was still talking to me. Perhaps I'd held it together better than I thought.

"I have little to say. Good or bad."

"He thought you were good-looking but not very nice," Jana injected, paused for effect, then added, "'Pretty, but a bitch,' were his exact words."

I cringed inwardly, then lashed out, "That is rich coming from a schmuck, and an American schmuck at that." The London fashion business was rich with Yiddish swear words. Jana ignored my outburst.

"Don't worry, I can salvage it," she said.

"Well, I am away on a modeling trip for the next two weeks, so he does not have to talk to me." This time I was the one who paused for effect and then added, "He never has to see me again."

"Oh, he wants to see you!" Jana assured me.

"Jana, please, stop meddling!"

"Where're you going?" she asked.

"To America." I knew the irony would not escape her.

During the trip, I forgot the whole incident. It was my first time in New York, and I fell in love with the City That Never Sleeps.

When I arrived back in England, winter was definitely over. The sun was shining and I was in a good mood.

"Hello." I answered the phone but did not recognize the voice on the other end of the line. I let the man talk to see if I could figure out who he was. Since I had just returned from America, the accent sounded less unusual than it otherwise would.

"I met you at Jana's birthday party," said the voice.

"Oh." I looked for the dots to connect.

"I am the guy you argued with," he said.

"Oh," I said again. Very articulate, I told myself. In an attempt to salvage some shred of my dignity, I said the first thing that came to my mind. "Do you want to go to the cinema?"

My own words shocked me and surprised Jim.

"Sure."

"What do you want to see?" I asked, knowing I was trapped.

"Oh God," he said.

"You don't have to go if you don't want to," I said.

"No, no." He laughed. "It's the name of the movie. *Oh God* with George Burns and John Denver."

We both laughed and, strangely, I was looking forward to the movie. I had never seen either actor in the movie, although I was a fan of John Denver's music.

After the night at the movies, we talked on the phone every day and went to the pub or theater or just ice cream. But not to dinner. That would be dating. One day Jim invited me to come and watch an episode of *Two's Company,* a TV show we both liked, in his flat. The show was about a no-nonsense, emancipated, American woman writer who lived in England, played by Elaine Stritch, and a witty, often cheeky butler played by Donald Sinden. I was curious to see what Jim's flat was like. The usual bachelor mess, I thought.

When I walked into his kitchen, my eyes fell on the corkboard and I was mesmerized. There were pictures of Jim's parents, his brothers and sisters, and, most importantly, all his nieces and nephews. On top of the board was a picture of the family's latest addition, his sister's newborn baby.

I decided on the spot I would marry him. I was twenty-eight years old and I knew exactly what qualities I was looking for in my partner. Being a family person was number one on my list. Things moved pretty fast after that.

We set the date and for a short time, like all young girls, I fell into a spell of wedding planning. For the first time I bought wedding magazines that did not have my picture in them and leafed through the pages filled with magnificent gowns. I imagined myself wearing them. It was very different than modeling the gowns. It was a dream every girl, no matter how briefly, entertained.

My parents applied for two exit visas, but only my father was allowed to go. So, once again the Communist regime back home crushed my dream and I lost my appetite for the dress and the party.

"What is the point of the party without family?" I said.

"Why don't we just elope?" said my soon-to-be husband.

"Okay." I agreed, mostly because I could not think why not.

The next morning, while I was eating breakfast, the phone rang.

"Go to my flat and in the bedroom in the left top drawer of the dresser is my passport. Take it and go to the Ealing registrar's office. They have an opening this Friday at ten a.m. Don't forget to bring your passport as well and your checkbook and get the wedding license." He spoke in a tone of voice as if he were giving me the train schedule. He paused, and then added, "I suppose you want to buy a dress. While you are shopping, you might as well get yourself a wedding band. I don't know what you like."

"Who said romance is dead?" I thought.

I tried to call home but had no luck. Sometimes it took several days of trying before I reached my family. So, I wrote them a letter and told them we moved the date of the wedding forward.

The night before we got married, Jim called his father and told him that he was getting married the next day. Since Jim was the youngest of six children, missing his son's wedding was not a huge disappointment to his father, or his mother, who hated to travel and was relieved she did not have to fly from Boston to London.

Jim's father had only one question. "Is she Catholic?"

"No," said Jim.

"C'est la vie," responded my future father-in-law.

My husband and my mother-in-law

the consequences of our choices

Like all young brides, I had visions of myself in a splendid wedding gown surrounded by family and friends. But travel out of Czechoslovakia was once again at the whim of an official, and that morning the official felt particularly spiteful and granted a visa only to my father. My mother's and my brothers' visas were declined. I was devastated. Jim was not much for the big wedding anyway and so he suggested we elope. My wedding dreams were gone so I agreed, and by the time my father arrived in London, I was married.

Jim and I took my father to a Greek restaurant for a mini celebration. I had noticed my father watching Jim turning his wedding band on his finger.

"What is wrong with his finger?" my father asked. I explained that his band was too big. "Really? Mine is too small," said my father, and before I knew what was happening, my father and my husband swapped their wedding bands. No translation necessary.

* * *

The weeks allocated to my father's visit in London flew by and I had a busy weekend planned for the three of us before my father's departure on Monday. My father was an early riser, so when I did not hear him moving around by eight a.m., I knocked on the door of his bedroom. Nothing. Slowly I opened the door and went in. My father was lying on the floor next to his bed. I touched his cheek. It was cold.

"I think my father is dead," I told my husband. We both stood in the hallway of our small apartment. Jim disappeared into the bedroom, and I waited for him to emerge, hoping he would tell me I was wrong, silly, crazy...Instead, he came out with his head down and held me in his arms.

In a daze, I went to our bedroom while Jim called an emergency number. I reached for my photo album, as if the pictures could bring my father back. There he was in a faded picture bent over a long table, cutting a piece of cloth with what I used to think when I was a child were giant scissors. Dad was not very tall, but he was always slim, and his hair was thick and black. He was not a vain man, but he was proud of his thick, dark hair.

I recognized the red dress he had made for me when I was five in the next picture. I wore it as he braided my hair.

And here he was, sneaking a fatty piece of pork onto my grandmother's plate. Grandma was my mum's mother. She lived with us for twelve years, as I described earlier. Most of the time, she was confined to bed. She prayed a lot and loved to eat everything the doctor told her not to eat. She had a special relationship with my father. I used to hang around with them a lot.

Here was Dad again hunched over a sewing machine threading the needle. He hated when the thread would break and often, forgetting that I was around, would swear at the thread, the factory, and the people who made the thread. I knew my grandma did not like it. She would start to pray.

One day, when he was in a big rush to finish a dress he'd promised to have ready for our neighbor's son's wedding, the thread broke more often than usual. He hated the Communists and blamed them for everything, including the bad weather. Dad burned the Communist factory with several four-letter words; he compared the Communist thread to unrepeatable subjects. The no-good Communist responsible for producing the inferior thread was sent to Communist purgatories peppered with a few more four-letter words. I hid in the corner, knowing he was furious.

Suddenly my grandma started to swear. Her thin, white hair fell over her kind, wrinkled face. Her weather-beaten hands, which generally rested folded on top, beat the duvet cover. She was worse than my dad.

My father stopped swearing and turned to face Grandma, who sat in her bed while the filthy words poured out of her mouth. Shocked, Dad asked her what she was doing. She looked at him with an innocent expression and said, "Helping you."

"How?" he asked.

"I will swear, and you sew," she said.

I never heard my father swear again, at least not around Grandma. I smiled at the memory.

And here I was about six years old, with my nose barely above the sewing machine table and Dad's dark, unruly eyebrows knotted in intense concentration. And at that moment, with my father lying dead in the next room, I realized that he would never learn the mystery of his cigarettes. I would never be able to tell him that he had not misplaced his half-smoked cigarettes. I would not say to him that because my mother complained that the sweater she had knitted for him smelled like a stale cigarette, I'd devised a plan. It was the simple plan of a six-year-old. I would reach for the cigarette he put on the side of the ashtray, and when he was not looking, take it outside, extinguish it, and then tear open the fragile paper with my fingernail and spread the tobacco in the garden under the weeds.

I wondered if my grandmother had seen me taking the cigarettes. She never said anything, maybe because she also hated him smoking. Suddenly a thought occurred to me. Had we been in a silent conspiracy? Overwhelming guilt shook me to the core, and at last, I could cry.

Jim knocked on the door and told me that the undertakers were going to take my father away. I did not come out. I wanted to remember him alive.

The next day we went to see the coroner. He was a small man about my father's age and build. He looked healthy, and I wondered with irrational jealousy why my father had to die while this man looked the picture of health.

"Your father was a remarkably healthy man," said the coroner. I thought he was making a cruel joke. I stared at him.

"He did not have cancer." He checked his papers again and then asked with interest, "Was your father a miner?"

I looked at him as if to say, "Are you mad?"

"He was a tailor," inserted my husband.

"I believe this belongs to you." The coroner handed me a small brown envelope.

I opened the envelope and out came the gold wedding band.

I held it in my hand and remembered the night my father and my new husband exchanged their wedding rings.

"Pity," I heard the coroner say. "If he did not smoke, he could have lived much longer."

I squeezed the wedding band in my hand.

Years later, my oldest son married his wife with a wedding band that first belonged to his father, then his grandfather, and finally to him. Third time lucky.

The night before my father died

when silence is not an option

"An Iron Curtain has descended across the continent," said Winston Churchill famously, as Europe became divided between East and West.

On the East side, government-controlled publications like *Pravda* were full of untruths, misinformation, and threats further spread by government-installed radio and television broadcasters. People relied on institutions like BBC World Service, Radio Free Europe, and Voice of America to shed light on what really was going on at home and abroad. After the brief interlude of Socialism with a Human Face put forth by Alexander Dubcek, and its subsequent, tragic end in August, 1968, Czechoslovakia fell into the iron grip of the Soviet Union.

My brother Jan was an English teacher and, as such, was suspect. The pressure to join the Communist Party was enormous. He retaliated by utilizing tapes recorded from the BBC in his classes, arguing that *Oliver Twist* was hardly Western propaganda. The party viewed this as a provocation. He was told to join the Communist Party and prove that he could be trusted to teach young minds the socialist ideals—or find a different job.

He'd thought about emigrating for a long time, but with two boys barely more than babies, it was too difficult. He watched the people who'd marched for Dubcek "turn their coats" (*otocit kabaty*), praising any order that came from Moscow. Truth was not an option.

In time, Jan's sons were no longer babies and he felt more and more suffocated by the Communist regime. At last, his wife agreed to leave. To pull it off, secrecy was of the utmost importance. A vacation in the "West" for his whole family was not allowed. But Jan saw a way. He would divide his family and ask for two separate permissions to travel. It was a complicated affair and relied on the Communists' incompetence.

Jan also had an important trump card up his sleeve. He had a sister who lived in London and was married to a US citizen.

Without any communication I could not be sure my brother Jan had pulled off his exit. When I saw him and his family walking towards me, I felt huge relief. Driving to my house, the boys, ages six and seven, took in the bustle of London. Their eyes were shining with excitement when they saw my refrigerator stocked with Coca-Cola. Not that I thought Coca-Cola was the best that the West had to offer, but it was not so long ago when my own eyes rolled in delight when I first tasted the dark, sweet liquid.

The quiet three-bedroom terrace house in Kew Gardens in

London was suddenly full of life. Soon the boys discovered the thirty-two flavors of Baskin-Robbins and their conversion was complete. They pronounced themselves English citizens.

My brother considered himself a political emigrant, but I knew it would take a while for him to get his papers, if at all. Unexpectedly, good fortune presented him with a job opening at the BBC World Service in the Czechoslovak section. For Jan, for whom the BBC World Service had been a lifeline to the truth, the opportunity was a stunning gift. His qualifications as a Slovak and English teacher were well suited for the job description. But there still were written tests and translation tests to be passed.

Our mother arrived for what was originally going to be the highlight of the summer: the birth of my first child. The decade was about to turn from the seventies to the eighties and I was about to turn thirty years old. I still had two weeks to go when my brother was invited to the BBC for his final test, the voice test.

My mother chewed her nails as I drove Jan toward the Strand. We watched him walk toward the Bush House at Aldwych from where the BBC World Service broadcasted. The job would almost certainly mean a work permit, not to mention security and good pay. But for my mother, it was much more.

"Imagine, my son a broadcaster for the BBC," she said to me after Jan disappeared into the building. I looked at her and she seemed to be sitting straighter; her face looked younger. I did not want to point out that it was going to make things difficult for her when she returned home. So, I nodded, and we kept our fingers crossed.

I saw my brother walking toward us, smiling. I let him tell our mother that indeed she did have a son who was a broadcaster for the BBC. We all hugged and my mother and I shed tears of joy.

I pictured my mother back in Czechoslovakia, in our small living room, with all her neighbors as they listened to her son on the radio. She would be in the center of the room, proud as a peacock.

My brother saw himself fighting the Communists by telling people at home the truth. He was dedicated to his work at the BBC and on weekends took a job in a restaurant. My sister-in-law cleaned houses and they saved rent money by living with us. There was no more Coca-Cola or ice cream for the boys, but the sacrifice was worth it, because before long they were able to buy a small house in Harrow on the outskirts of London.

* * *

The London Underground stopped running at midnight, so when Jan had his late-night broadcast at the BBC, he would ride his bicycle home. He was still saving for his first car. He was approaching the last leg of his journey one night, when out of nowhere a car came behind him at full speed, blinding him for just a few seconds, and then everything went dark. He lay on the street until a good Samaritan called the police from a nearby telephone booth and he was transported to the hospital.

For the next few days his life hung by a thread. The weeks turned into months, and he was still suffering with headaches and double vision when I came to visit. He joked that he always wanted to have two sisters.

Eventually he came home from the hospital. The reality was, my brother was very lucky to be alive. As a child he was always very skinny. "Skin and bones," my mother would lament. But the doctor told him, "If you were even a few pounds heavier, your own weight would have broken your neck."

"You know . . ." Jan said, one day when we sat sharing some tea. He seemed to be mentally debating if he should tell me. "About a week before the accident, one of my colleagues," he refused to tell me who, "told me that when he was on a vacation in Yugoslavia, he was accosted by the KGB."

I felt a stab in my stomach.

"They wanted him to report everything that went on at the BBC. He called MI6, and they told him to give them some useless information."

My palms began to sweat.

"He thought telling them I ride my bike home after work was pretty useless."

"Except it wasn't." I finished for him. "You should quit the BBC; you'll find a different job."

"That is exactly what they are after. Control by fear," he said.

I cursed Brezhnev, and I prayed in my agnostic heart that there would never be a leader of a powerful nation who would be able to spread falsehoods and untruth, and mobilize followers in his own perverse ideology, and have men who know better fear him enough to harm others just to gain favor with him. An unfortunate prophecy, as it turned out, but on that day, all those years ago, I was just thankful my brother had survived the attack.

"Besides, they cannot kill us all." Jan interrupted my mental prayer. When the doctor gave him the all clear, Jan went back to work at the BBC World Service.

My brother would not be silenced.

When Silence Is Not an Option was published by **Nixes Mate Review**. Issue 18, Winter 2021

going home

Pushing my mother in the wheelchair with one hand and the stroller with my eighteen-month-old son with the other, I hurried through the long corridors of the airport making sure I got to my gate on time. After the flight attendant helped me wheel my mother onto the plane, I settled my son in a seat next to the window and my mother in the aisle seat. I sat in the middle.

My son fell asleep as soon as the plane was in the air and my mother shortly after. On our way to the airport, I saw a letter addressed to me that I had put in my handbag. I took it out, but I did not recognize the handwriting or the return address on the envelope. The card inside was a sympathy card.

"Pearl gave me your address and asked me to write to you in the event of her death. As you know, she was sick for some time," wrote a woman named Alice. "I was her friend and neighbor. She talked about you often and with such love, which is why

I am so deeply saddened to tell you that Pearl Landis passed away..."

I closed my eyes and let the tears flow down my cheeks. I held my mother's hand and when she woke up, I told her about Mrs. Landis's passing. She looked upward and said, "You did a great job looking after my girl. Thank you. I see you soon."

"Not too soon," I said.

We held hands during the hour-long flight.

"I am proud of you," my mother said unexpectedly. My family was not much into praise in term of words. My mother was more likely to talk a neighbor's ear off about my success, rather than praise me directly. I did not know what to say so I just squeezed her hand and looked out the window, watching the earth get closer and the noise louder as the plane landed.

After negotiating the corridors of Prague's airport, we boarded a much smaller airplane that would take us to our little town, called Piestany. My mother was frozen by fear, while my son squealed with delight.

At last, we arrived home. After everyone went to bed, my brother Pavel made some cooked wine and garlic bread.

"So, what is going on?" he asked, putting the garlic bread and the hot wine in front of me.

"She is deaf," I said.

"What, why, how?" asked Pavel.

Let me start from the beginning...

* * *

My mother came to London to spend Christmas with me before we left for Hong Kong, where we were moving for a few years because of my husband's business. I would take a pause from modeling work in London and resume when we came back, or so went the plan. Knowing my mother's thirst for travel, to take her to Hong Kong was an irresistible dream and I was determined to fulfill it. I started the process of getting her visa. The long paperwork and endless lines would be challenging even without a sick woman and fidgeting child. But we did it.

While we waited for the paperwork to come back, I packed. My husband was already working in Hong Kong and was getting the apartment there ready for our arrival. My mother's task was the hardest. She fought the illness that was mercilessly closing in on her. Each engrossed in our individual tasks, we did not pay enough attention to each other. Until my mother fell off her bed trying to get up. I called an ambulance and she was put in the ICU.

Her visa was rejected. I canceled the airline tickets. They would not let my child into the ICU. I was being torn to shreds but falling apart was not an option. I kept smiling at my mother and at my child. When my mother was moved to a hospital bed, I bought her strawberries. She wanted me to take a picture with her and the strawberries. It was February and at home she would not be able to see strawberries in the middle of winter, let alone eat them. I smiled at the gusto with which she was devouring the strawberries, and some of my hope had come back.

The doctor called me to his office.

"You need to take your mother home as soon as possible." There was something in the way he said it that made the denied visa seemed irrelevant.

"She will lose her hearing," said the doctor. "The only way we were going to be able to get your mother out of the ICU was by using a drug which has side effects."

"Is it permanent?" I asked.

"Yes."

"But she can hear me. Not well, but she can hear me." I was looking at the doctor, willing him to give me some hope.

"I advise you to take your mother home as soon as you can. We will give her medication to make the journey possible." The doctor seemed cold, but I understood. I brought my mother home from the hospital and booked our airline tickets for the day after. The next day, however, we went shopping and I bought my mother a beautiful dress and then took her to the best restaurant that would allow a child in. We had ice cream with my son then sat on a bench and played a game of who can find something funny about people passing by. For a while we had fun.

After a pause, my mother said, "Where is Frank Zappa?" Then answered herself, "Gone." We went home; people no longer looked funny.

"How long?" Pavel's question brought me out of the story I was telling.

"I don't know."

I stayed a week, then went back to London and from there to Hong Kong. As usual my mother defied death for a while longer. Three months to be precise when the inevitable news arrived, I held the telegram in my hand while my eyes filled with tears. The letters began to swim and dance until they became unrecognizable.

I remembered the day my mother had the original surgery for uterine cancer. I came to visit her in the hospital and to my delight she looked the same. She was forty-six years old and full of vigor.

"You are going to England," she said. "I will be fine. Your dad is here and your brothers are here. I don't want you to think about changing your plans." She did not look ill and I knew if she wanted me to go, I would go.

It was the beginning of a roller-coaster that lasted thirteen years. She buried her healthy husband, which was as devastating as it was unexpected. But she knew that unlike her husband, she was given many chances and she was not going to waste them. She found a reason to live and she fought hard and enjoyed every day. She made sure that when the day came and she inevitably lost the long battle, she would have no regrets.

I looked down at the tear-stained telegram. Only a few months ago she was planning to go to Hong Kong. Now she was taking her final journey to meet her partner and the love of her life.

"I am glad she had those strawberries," I said to my husband, who sat next to me while I processed the information on the brown piece of paper. Without knowing the details, he understood.

storms

I watched the London lights disappear under me as the plane headed toward Hong Kong. My son, Jimmy, was soon fast asleep as our journey had started at night. I settled in my seat and opened my book. *Noble House* by James Clavell.

The first time I traveled to the Far East, as a model, it was a three-week trip to Singapore, Hong Kong, Tokyo, and Kyoto. Everything was new and exciting. I wrote lots of postcards to my family, especially my mother, who I knew had her atlas open and traveled with me. My second trip was a ten-day trip to Hong Kong to shoot a TV commercial. On that trip I read James Clavell's *Tai Pan*. There was so much I wanted to see. I befriended a local model who showed me around, and the scenes from the book came alive.

When the reality of living in Hong Kong materialized, of course the first thing I thought of was to walk in Wan Chai with my mother, but it was not to be.

My husband and I settled in a small apartment close to Wan Chai. We wanted to experience real Hong Kong life, not the expatriate's life. I contacted an agent I met on my previous visit and did some modeling, but mostly I immersed myself in exploring Hong Kong and soon I was looking forward to the arrival of my second child.

The typhoon, *Tai Fung*, as the storm is called in Cantonese, was approaching Hong Kong, and many vessels were seeking refuge in Victoria Harbor. Expatriates, as well as the local population, were bracing for what was to come.

Although the storm was not close enough to prevent my husband from going to work, two-year-old Jimmy and I were marooned inside the apartment building under Victoria Peak. I was seven months pregnant, so Jimmy and I spent the morning reading *Mr. Men* books.

The sky looked ominous as I walked into the kitchen, followed by Jimmy.

"Can I have eggs for lunch?"

"No, you had an egg for breakfast."

"But I want to be strong like Mr. Strong. Strong by name, strong by nature. And you know what his secret is? Eggs." Jimmy quoted his favorite book, *Mr. Strong*.

"You will have spinach so that you can be strong like Popeye."

"But I want to be strong like Mr. Strong!" My little man stood his ground.

"I have to run to the bathroom now. Then I will show you the book about Popeye."

"Can I have more juice?" he asked.

I filled his sippy cup, then poured myself a hot coffee and waddled out of the kitchen toward the bathroom.

I was washing my hands when I heard our helper Catherine's cry, *"Ei-Yahh!"* ringing out from the kitchen. I hurried in to find Catherine wiping the floor. Jimmy was standing next to the table, my coffee cup turned on its side, the hot liquid still dripping from the table onto the floor. His face and clothes were wet.

Instinctively, I took off his clothes, wrapped him up in a large towel, and dialed the emergency number. I was told that because of the approaching storm, it would take at least an hour before an ambulance could reach us.

I grabbed my car keys and, carrying the shocked little boy in my arms, I told Catherine to walk with me to the car.

"Call my husband and tell him what happened and tell him to meet me at the hospital."

I secured Jimmy in the car. He was quiet, and his face looked almost normal. For a moment I allowed myself to hope that it would not be too bad after all.

"Drive carefully," I heard Catherine say as I pulled out of our building's underground garage.

The wind and the rain hit the windshield with such vengeance I winced instinctively and dug my nails into the steering wheel. I steadied the car and adjusted to the onslaught of rain. Going through the town was not an option. I had to go over the mountain. I had done the drive on my way to the hospital for prenatal visits. The narrow, winding road was usually busy with people admiring the stunning view of Kowloon and the Victoria Harbour below, but I was certain that today the road would be empty.

Seventh-Day Adventist Hospital, where I was heading, was popular among expatriates. I'd chosen the obstetrician because he was trained at the Queen Charlotte Hospital in London, where Jimmy was born.

Controlling my urge to speed, I climbed up Peak Road. As I suspected, there were no other cars in sight. I reached the crossroads: the right fork would take me to the Peak, and the left would take me to the hospital, half a mile down Stubbs Road. Just as I started to descend toward the hospital, the windshield wipers stopped working. I stuck my head out of the window into the wind and rain, and slowly drove the car down to the hospital.

I covered Jimmy's face with the extra towel I'd brought with me, and, carrying my precious cargo, I ran through the rain toward the emergency door. Two nurses ran toward us. One of them took Jimmy gently out of my arms, and the other gave me a towel and led me into the treatment room.

I peppered the doctor with questions. The answers were designed to keep me calm, and I was desperate to believe them.

"We'll have to keep him here for a few days," the doctor said when he was finished.

My little boy was bandaged from neck to waist, and I couldn't see his left hand at all. The left half of his face was shining with something, but I couldn't tell what. I held his good hand while we wheeled him into a hospital room.

My husband arrived, and the iron cage that had been holding me together disintegrated. I collapsed into his arms and cried uncontrollably. The nurse came in and took me downstairs to my obstetrician's office.

"You have to take care of your baby," she said.

"So why are you taking me away from him?" I asked, sobbing.

"Your unborn baby." She pointed at my stomach.

"Oh," I said, connecting back to reality.

After the unscheduled ultrasound, I was told that—so far—all was well.

Hospital regulations demanded that Jimmy sleep in a bed with side protection. I pushed my bed next to his crib and watched my little boy sleep.

I wished I could turn back the clock, or at least those few seconds when I poured the cup of coffee. My heart broke into a thousand pieces, and my guilt threatened to suffocate me.

I watched one side of Jimmy's face and neck swell and fill with liquid. The coffee had burned his lips and his tongue, making it painful for him to eat or drink. The doctor inserted an IV. I fell into despair. The nurses got accustomed to me wandering through the corridors of the hospital.

One night, I wandered into the hospital chapel. I knew very little about Seventh-Day Adventist beliefs other than they were vegetarian, and did not smoke, or drink alcohol or coffee. I kneeled and prayed. I felt a bit better. My grandmother was right. There was only one God for all religions and he would hear us no matter where we are.

I put both my hands on my belly and felt my baby kick. I stroked my unborn child as he/she seemed to be playing soccer inside my stomach. I knew I could no longer indulge in guilt; both my children needed me.

With time, the bandages started to shrink. My little boy's beautiful face healed first. The large bandages on his arm became small wrist wraps, and I could see his belly button again.

We read a lot of books.

Dr. Yei asked me to bring my husband to his office the next time he came to the hospital. We had been living in the hospital for more than six weeks and finally there was hope that we might be able to go home.

"Jimmy is progressing so well that I can start the grafting next week," the doctor told us.

"What?" I asked.

"After a burn, we often need to do a graft. This means taking skin from an unaffected area and grafting it onto the burned area," explained Dr. Yei. "With someone as young as Jimmy, I hope to be successful in making the scars almost invisible."

I dismissed "almost" and hung onto "invisible."

"If you agree, I'd like to start next week," continued the doctor. "When is the baby due?"

"In four weeks," I said.

"Well then, the sooner we start, the better."

"Where will you take the skin from?" asked my husband.

"From his leg," Dr. Yei said. "After the graft, Jimmy will have more pain from the giver area than from the grafted area."

"Nothing to eat or drink after eight p.m.," said the nurse the night before Jimmy's first graft. Jimmy loved his sippy cup. To convince him to go to sleep without a drink was hard. I cleared the room of anything that could remind him of a drink.

The first words I heard in the morning were, "Mummy, I'm thirsty." It was seven a.m. His surgery was scheduled for nine thirty. I refused to have a drink, in solidarity. By nine a.m., my voice was hoarse from reading Jimmy his favorite books.

In the waiting room in front of the operating theater, Jimmy sat on my lap, what was left of it, still saying, "I'm thirsty."

After the surgery, I watched my son slowly emerge from his artificial sleep. There were no bandages on his wrist or his elbow anymore, but now, his left thigh was bandaged down to his knee. Slowly he opened his eyes and asked for his sippy cup.

"I'm thirsty."

His voice was small, and I held my breath, preparing to say, "Not yet," but he closed his eyes again.

When he woke up about an hour later, he focused his eyes on me. "Mummy, I'm thirsty."

The doctor said to hold off giving him liquids as long as possible; well, I couldn't hold off anymore. I helped him sit up and gave him his sippy cup. He drank half the liquid in the cup and almost instantly threw up. But then, thankfully, he went back to sleep.

The next time he woke up, I told him that he could drink out of my glass because he was such a brave boy. The glass made it easier for me to guide him into taking only small sips. This time, he did not throw up. Slowly, with pauses as long as I managed to negotiate, Jimmy drank the full glass and kept all its contents inside him. I hoped he would not have to go through the ordeal again, but of course, he did. But, each time a part of the bandages came off, the sun shined a little brighter.

"How is your little boy doing?" the obstetrician asked on my next visit.

"Recovering from another graft," I said.

"You know a birth ten days before the delivery date is considered a full-term."

"What's wrong?" I learned to read between the lines.

"The baby's heartbeat is a little slower than I would like it to be."

"When?" I asked.

"Tomorrow."

"I'll let my husband know," I said and left the office.

I was ready for the doctor at 6:00 a.m. After all, I did not have far to go. I was still living in Jimmy's hospital room. I kissed Jimmy and promised him he would have a brother by the end of the day.

I settled into a hospital room two floors below the pediatrics and waited for the pain to come. I was determined not to have an epidural. For a while I felt only minor pain. But when it did come, it came with a vengeance. I welcomed every brutal stab without protest. There's nothing like enduring physical pain to ease lingering guilt. Several hours later, an eternity to me, the doctor decided to see how I was doing.

"I would like to give you something to help you to speed up the process."

"As long as it is not an epidural," I said.

"It is not." The doctor gave me an injection, and I fell asleep.

When I woke up, I did not know where I was. I felt an overwhelming sense of responsibility. I knew I had something important to do.

"Doctor. I have something terribly important to do," I said, "but I cannot remember what it is."

"You are going to have a baby," the doctor replied.

If I had been able to comprehend the conversation, I would have overheard him say to my husband in an aside, "This reaction is extremely rare."

"Will she get back to normal?"

"Yes, as soon as the drug wears off."

Before the doctor left, I told him one more time that I had something terribly important to do, but I couldn't remember what it was. I closed my eyes. I felt the needle going into my spine, but I had no idea how much time had elapsed when I heard the doctor say, "We're good to go."

My bed was moving down the corridor. I watched the nurse who walked with us hand the gurney upon which I lay to another nurse who pushed me into a very cold room. I thought the new nurse had an awful sense of fashion. She was covered from head to toe with ill-fitting clothing. I had never seen any nurse dressed like that.

Two men who looked like Egyptian mummies walked in.

"Let's get this baby out."

I recognized my doctor's voice.

"Push!" said the doctor.

I did as I was told. The other man I now recognized as my husband. I don't know how long it had been going on when the doctor said something to the nurse then rather loudly to me: "Push!" The nurse leaned her whole weight on my stomach. I could feel the pain, and then I felt the baby come out.

I sensed palpable tension and commotion going on at the foot of my bed. My husband covered my eyes. Somebody took the baby away. I thought it was strange, but my mind was hazy, and I didn't dwell on it. The doctor told us we had a baby boy and I felt relieved and promptly fell asleep.

The next morning, the doctor came into my room. He sat next to my bed.

"The reason you were in the operating room (*I was in an operating room?!*) was because we knew the baby was in distress, and you may have needed an emergency C-section. Earlier on you had an unexpected reaction to the medication, which made the C-section risky, so we did our best to avoid it. It was touch-and-go for a while. We kept your baby in the ICU for the night, but you can see him now."

The baby looked tiny in his hospital cot, yet, somehow very determined. We named him Daniel Martin. I loved the name. We took Jimmy to see his brother and he could not wait to play with him.

Finally, the day came when the doctor took off the last of Jimmy's bandages and the whole family came back to the apartment I'd left four months earlier. It was May, and after a season of storms both literal and metaphorical, it was the month of love and hope for our family.

It also made my new baby a Taurus. To say that my Taurus was an early riser would be an understatement. At 4:00 a.m. he was hungry and, after being fed, refused to go back to sleep. Afraid to wake up Jimmy, who was still recuperating from his ordeal, I would take Danny out for a walk. For many months, my son and I walked on deserted roads in a section of Hong Kong Island called the Mid-Levels. It was a residential area carved into the side of Victoria Peak. It was indeed halfway between the valley at the foot of the mountain that housed most of Hong Kong's businesses, and its peak. We looked down at the spectacular Hong Kong harbor and watched the waking city get drenched in a powerful subtropical sun.

Hong Kong was ceded by China to Britain after the first opium war in 1842. But it was not until 1899, after another opium war, that the Quning dynasty leased the so-called New Territories to the United Kingdom for ninety-nine years....and that time was running out.

Despite the fact that we left Hong Kong for America when my Taurus was just three years old, he had a somewhat romantic attachment to his birthplace. Years later, on July 1, 1997, on a flagpole that usually sported an American flag, my son hoisted the colonial flag of Hong Kong and stayed up all night to witness the return of Hong Kong and the New Territories to China. As Prince Charles watched the last ceremony being performed in the British colony, at 4:00 a.m. US time, in the sleeping suburbs of New Jersey and with the help of the TV, my son lowered the Hong Kong flag from the flagpole in sync with the one being lowered over the governor's house in Hong Kong. He folded it gently and put it in a special box that he had prepared for it. Finally, he felt fully American. The country of his birth was no more.

Jimmy eventually healed as much as the injury of that type can. Every summer, however, when I saw his scars, I felt the matching set in my heart. My son, however, used his scars as a screening device. He told me if a girl was put off by his scars, she was not worth talking to. What he did not tell me was that he also used his scars as a sympathy magnet. Eventually he married the perfect girl. She did not see the scars at all.

boston

The official took my passport and led me away from my family into an office marked "Immigration Officer."

Our family of four entered the United States at the Chicago airport. We flew in from Hong Kong and, because our younger son suffered from high-altitude ear sensitivity, the journey proved to be tiring indeed. Danny's pain and his crying had multiplied exponentially once we were airborne. I spent thirteen long hours trying to console the suffering little boy, and to keep his crying at as low a level as possible, while avoiding accusatory looks from my fellow passengers.

"I will wait for you on the other side," I heard my husband say as I watched him walk away with our two sons toward the sign "US Citizens Only."

I knew all my papers were in order, as I had done the extensive application ritual at the US embassy in Hong Kong. I followed the immigration officer into a small office. He told me I could sit down and then he left, I assumed to get more paperwork. I leaned my head against the wall and promptly fell asleep.

The immigration officer coughed to wake me up. Seeing my groggy and I am sure confused look, he offered me the cup of coffee that he had probably brought for himself. After I answered all his questions, I was able to join my family and together we flew to Boston, our new home.

Life in New England was very different from the life I was used to in London or Hong Kong. We bought a house on Beacon Hill because the area reminded us of London and Prague. The old brick houses surrounding Louisville Square, the gaslights and cobblestone streets, made us feel at home. My husband bought me a book called *Beacon Hill, Hub of the Universe.* As the book pointed out, Beacon Hill's life was like no other. It was part snobbish, part traditional, part liberal, and a good deal eccentric.

I loved the physical beauty of Boston and Beacon Hill but I did not exactly fit in. My accent assured me a designated place in people's minds and it made me feel uncomfortable.

There were several reasons why I failed to feel at home in Boston. Right at the beginning I started off on the wrong foot. I assumed life in America would be the same as in England; if anything would be different, I felt sure, it would be for the better. I assumed in America, like in England, there was a National Health Service. Even in Czechoslovakia, where healthcare left a lot to be desired, as I knew only too well, it was available to all. I learned the contrary the hard way.

My son Danny suffered with ear infections. The first time I needed a doctor, needless to say, happened when my husband was out of the country on business. I called the pediatrician's office I found in the Yellow Pages and before I could say anything, I was asked what insurance I had.

"What?" I asked. The conversation after that did not go well. I called my husband.

"Tell them you will pay cash." I did and that conversation went even worse.

I called eight pediatricians, by which time I was crying and begging. Finally, a Good Samaritan on the other end of the phone suggested I take my son to the hospital's emergency room. It had never occurred to me to go to an emergency room because in my mind, emergency rooms were only for emergencies. However, by then it had become an emergency for me too.

Perhaps my difficulty fitting in in Boston was not just that I wanted Boston to look like London; perhaps it was because I was looking for the life I had in London. I also missed the international melting pot of friends I met in Hong Kong. Meanwhile, we spent every weekend in our house on Cape Cod, not giving Boston a chance to show us its charm. After a year we convinced ourselves that we were not yet ready to close the circle of our travels and create a permanent home. Our gypsy feet took us to Monte Carlo.

It was not the first time for either one of us to visit the tiny principality. We had each spent time in Monaco before we met, both for leisure and for work. We both loved the food, the weather, and the international atmosphere. We also spent our brief three-day honeymoon in Monte Carlo. While on our honeymoon, we had mused that Monaco would be an idyllic place to live.

Although we did have fun eating ourselves through the Mediterranean, we soon realized that our boys were misplaced. They went to an American School, which further isolated them from their surroundings. Reluctantly we came to the conclusion that just like holiday romances rarely translated to everyday life, honeymoon destinations did not make successful relocation homes.

After a long and honest discussion, we came to the conclusion that it was time to put our roots down. It was less of an epiphany than a reality that we were no longer free spirits. We were parents and we needed a permanent home for our family. We decided to move back to England.

I was looking forward to going back to London and to connect with my friends and perhaps pick up some threads of my abandoned career. However, at the last minute, a business opportunity came up for my husband and we relabeled our boxes to be sent to the US, New Jersey, to be precise.

a place for us

Suburbs! I could not believe it. My partner in adventure, my best friend, my husband wanted us to live in the New Jersey suburbs. The mere idea struck dread in my heart. I was always a city girl. Though I was born in a small town with a rich history and with a deep cultural tradition, even there, I had longed for a bigger city.

In my early teens, I would take an overnight train to Prague and wander around the bustling city. I could feel the pulse of the city life deep inside me. Even the sound of a siren was exciting. I seldom heard it back home because few people had cars, so the ambulance would have a clear path to the hospital. In Prague, the streets were full of trams, buses, and cars, and so the siren wailed often. It was sobering to know that the very sound could mean the difference between life and death to an unknown person. But being so very young, that thought kept me down only for a few short minutes.

I derived energy from walking through Wenceslas Square. The history was everywhere, and the future when one is fourteen years old is all achievable. I loved the fact that I was invisible, that nobody noticed me. It gave me a sense of freedom. Unlike at home where, if I walked barefoot on the bridge over the river Vah, imitating the British singer Sandie Shaw, my mother knew about it before I arrived home. And there were no telephones!!

Communism had its occasional advantages. A teenager like me could afford tickets to most theaters, where I would sit mesmerized. Sometimes I had to leave early and rush to the railway station to make the overnight train back home. I did not mind standing in the overcrowded train, on my way to Prague, because the excitement of going to the city pumped up my adrenaline and I didn't need sleep. Whether I was standing or sitting on my way back, I would be smiling with my eyes closed, leaving the fellow passengers to wonder about my mental status. In retrospect, what they were more likely wondering was, "Where is that girl's mother?"

The truth would have shocked them. My mother had no idea that I was not at my friend's house just a few towns over. This was possible because although within the town, news could travel fast, from town to town, not so much, and of course, there were no telephones. Also, I did actually stop on my way back and visit my friend to give her and me some cover and tell her of my new exploits. I "visited my friend Magda" as often as I dared.

But now, New Jersey...and the suburbs.

* * *

Practice makes perfect, they say, so given that we had moved six times in the first eight years of our marriage, my husband and

I had developed a routine. To make the task of unpacking more pleasant, after our boxes arrived, the first thing we would unpack and connect would be our stereo system. We found that after we turned the radio to a local station, we would learn about the weather as well as various upcoming events, not to mention have some music to lift us up.

And so, in our new house in the New Jersey suburbs, my husband connected the last wire, and out of the well-placed speakers came the clear voice of Barbra Streisand declaring, "There's a place for us..."

suburbs

I was not a candidate for the women's Junior League for the obvious reason that I did not go to school in the US. Nor did I play tennis. Two major ways to meet people in the suburbs. And since we were new to the neighborhood, we did not belong to any club, another way to make friends. Kind of a Catch-22. You had to be introduced by friends to get accepted to any club, but if you were new in town, how did you make friends? Children to the rescue!

I had two sons and soon another child was on the way. Since we arrived in March, Jimmy, my older son, was forced to step into his first grade about two-thirds through the year. Poor Jimmy, I really had no clue. I sent him off to school in a crisply ironed, light blue, Oxford shirt, dark blue wool pants, and leather shoes. If I had added jacket and tie, he would have been a miniature copy of his father going off to his office. The boy who loved school suddenly lost his enthusiasm. After what must have been a very long three days for seven-year-old Jimmy, I got a phone call from his school.

"Mrs. Sullivan, may I ask where are you from?" said the school nurse as a way of hello.

"Why?" I asked, defensive shields up.

"In the United States, we send our children to school in t-shirts and either jeans or sweatpants. Most importantly, the children wear sneakers. Could you—"

"Absolutely not!" I interrupted her. It would be highly disrespectful to the teacher for my son to go to school looking like a slob, and sneakers! They make everybody's feet smell!

"Mrs.—"

"Goodbye," I said.

I was shaking. I could not wait to tell my husband. Remembering the incident now makes me cringe and silently I ask for my son's forgiveness. I made the poor child go to school looking like an alien from a different planet, or in this case, a different continent, for another week. But his tears one afternoon when he came home from school put *my* behind in the seat of the car and we went shopping. Sensing my vulnerability, Jimmy got all the Lego he always wanted and then some. That crash course on burbs living showed me that close-mindedness can be on both sides. I opened my mind and started to settle in.

My second phone call in the burbs went much better than my first. It came from a neighbor called Nancy who informed me that her son was going to the Montessori school, which my younger son Danny was attending, and could we and the boys meet.

The first time I met Nancy, I knew I had met a true friend. Softly spoken, petite in stature with dark curly hair, she turned heads with her exotic looks. I was delighted when I realized that her mother was Spanish with an honest-to-goodness accent rivaling mine. I felt comfortable around her.

The first group Nancy introduced me to was the Twig #4. Twig was a group of friends that came together to support the local hospital. There was no specific time or fundraising commitment, but what I especially liked was that we could decide how the money we raised would be used. One year I remember our money went to support siblings of children who had terminal illnesses. So often the siblings of sick children are neglected. Not deliberately, it is just a fact. The parents have only so many resources and after all, there are only twenty-four hours in a day. So, we would pay for an outing to Six Flags Great Adventure Park. For that one afternoon those children were allowed to forget about their siblings and were told to have fun without guilt. It was painfully little, but it was better than nothing.

The first year I was involved in the Twig fundraising we bought an incubator for the pediatric department and when my daughter was born, at The Overlook Hospital, I was able to see the incubator. Thankfully, she did not need it, although I would need the hospital not long afterwards.

Out of the Twig group a smaller group of neighbors had formulated and got together every Mother's Day. We would rotate houses and on Mother's Day Sunday, the men would cook and, most importantly, clean up afterwards! We had several closet chefs among the group who would plan weeks, even month ahead THE MENU. The children, most of whom knew each other through school and sports, joined us. The lesser cooks were designated to cook hot dogs and hamburgers for the kids. The last group of men would be designated for the cleanup. Although they were all supposed to rotate, only the kids' cooks and the cleanup crew seemed to adhere to the unwritten rule. The CHEFS seemed to stay at their posts.

As for the women, we did nothing on Mother's Day, but we had plenty to discuss. Most of us belonged to the local Garden Club as well. We were the rejects of the prestigious Garden Club of America. Being a reject appealed to my reverse snobbery and added depth to the green color of my imaginary picture of the burbs.

Through all the groups around our town, the thread binding us was Nancy. She would also be the friend who would visit me in the hospital and bring me chocolate roses after my hysterectomy, when I needed all the support I could get.

Long after I moved away and our children grew up, our friendship did not fade. Most people send cards for Christmas, but Nancy never forgets my birthday. A friend indeed.

the gift of life

Like all new mothers, I felt content as I held my four-week-old daughter. She looked beautiful, nursing eagerly, building her strength to face the world.

"Your obstetrician called when you were out," said my husband on his way out to play with our two boys. The phone rang just as the door closed behind him.

"Your postnatal test came back, and you have cancer but you are not going to die." The doctor said the two sentences without a pause. But the only thing I heard was: *You have cancer.*

Mechanically I lay my daughter in her crib. Memory flooded in. My mother died of uterine cancer one month after her sixtieth birthday. She fought thirteen years against the faceless foe with tenacity and humor. And books. She loved to say that the cancer did not have a library card. As long as she could read, the cancer was kept out of her orbit.

I was thirty-seven, ten years younger than my mother was

when she was diagnosed. Did that mean that my battle would be longer, or that my life would be shorter?

The boys came in from the garden and my husband reminded me that we had to go to my uncle's wake. I nodded, but my mind was filled with smoky fog. I watched the boys having dinner bickering over nothing as boys that age do, spilling the food over the table. Somehow the mess made me feel better. It reminded me that life often is messy.

I recounted my conversation with the doctor to my husband. But where I only heard, "You have cancer," my husband heard, *you are not going to die.*

"You don't have to go to your uncle's wake if you don't feel up to it," he said.

"But I do," I said.

My mother used to say that Slovaks may miss the wedding, but they always came to pay their last respects. There was no way I was going to miss my uncle's wake.

At the wake I met family I had not seen in a long time and for a while forgot about myself. My cousin was there with her two daughters, and I was reminded that one of them, Susie, worked at the Sloan Kettering cancer research hospital in New York. I told her about my diagnosis.

"It'll reassure you to get a second opinion," said Susie, and offered to make an appointment for me at her hospital. The next day she called with the date and time.

* * *

The early morning darkness had begun to turn from espresso to cappuccino when I pulled into the empty parking lot of the Saks

Fifth Avenue department store. I had arranged to meet my friend Katrina there, because she could never navigate the complicated web of streets in the town where I lived.

I parked my car and stepped into an empty parking lot. I breathed in the icy January air. Abruptly, the headlights of an oncoming car blinded me. The music coming out of the car grew louder as it drew closer. By the time my friend Katrina's fire-engine-red Jeep pulled next to me, I could hear the Beatles declare: "I want to hold your hand."

I stepped inside the Jeep and was greeted by my friend's excited voice. "I made it in thirty minutes," she said triumphantly. I smiled and settled into the passenger seat.

I asked Katrina to go with me to Sloan Kettering because I needed to be with someone who had known me a very long time. Katrina turned the volume of the car radio even louder and let the music fill the car as she drove toward the city. I closed my eyes and let my mind wander back to the carefree times when Katrina and I worked together.

We had met on the set of a Close-Up toothpaste commercial in Frankfurt. Modeling as a job did not lend itself to long or deep friendships, yet Katrina and I stayed in touch. Fifteen years later, on the other side of the Atlantic, we found ourselves living in New Jersey's neighboring towns only forty minutes from each other.

Katrina still dressed to turn heads. Her flowing outfits hugged her slim body. With disregard for the season of the year, she always wore her outfits made out of smooth, silky fabric in hues of white and cream.

Her exuberance lifted everyone's spirits while her sparkling earrings danced around her dainty ears, never failing to deliver their cheerful message. The delicate chiffon scarf slid onto her neck as it gave up its attempt to cover her sunny, unruly hair with its tame-me-if-you-can attitude.

Katrina was as flamboyant as Oscar Wilde and as free as mustangs on the prairie, completely unique. It made perfect sense for us to meet at a top fashion department store. No other parking lot would have sufficed. I wished I did not have to open my eyes and let the image go.

As I followed the nurse down the long hospital corridor, I clung to my friend's *Forget Me Not* scent. It stayed with me during the long day of tests, uncertainty, and fear. When I finally came out of the doctor's office, into the crowded waiting room, Katrina was in a chair with her back to the door. Sitting straight, her spine barely brushing the back of her chair.

"After the surgery, you should be fine," said the doctor with a reassuring smile. "There will be no more children, but you *will*..." He put an emphasis on the word, "...be able to watch your children grow up."

Katrina turned and read my face with a perfection awarded to those who think through their heart.

"You will be fine!" she whispered and squeezed my hand. We walked in silence to the hospital parking lot. I knew it took willpower for her not to shout at the top of her lungs and celebrate because she knew that some people in that waiting room would not be as lucky. What Katrina lacked in understatement, she made up for in sensitivity.

When we reached her Jeep, Katrina held my hand and danced with me around the car. Her laugh seemed to have come from the center of her heart, but to me, it sounded like church bells ringing in a new life.

no regrets

My mother and I had traveled to Prague all those years ago because she believed that "Travel is the university of life."

"Two rooms?" asked the clerk at the hotel check-in desk.

"No, just one. This is my daughter." For an unknown reason my mother added, "She is still a child."

The clerk, his hair thinning even though he was quite young, peered at me over his spectacles and said, in a matter-of-fact voice, "Yes, still a child, but already interesting." I was thirteen years old, tall, skinny with no breasts in sight, but I understood that I had received my first compliment. I decide to live up to it.

The energy of the city intoxicated me. While my mother did her best to get me excited about Prague's historical sights, I was focused on the future. When the sound of an ambulance siren interrupted our conversation, my mother sighed in regret at the possibility of a life lost. To me the sound signaled the hope of life saved. I resolved to aim for life without regrets.

"Non je ne regrettte rien," I sang with Edith Piaf on my transistor radio.

We returned home to my little town in southern Czechoslovakia. I finished my education and eventually my breasts appeared.

I left, to travel and to learn. Soon after, Soviet tanks rolled down the Wenceslas Square and I would never live in my homeland again.

I went from sleeping in a London telephone booth at the railway station to magazine covers and film, even becoming a Bond Girl. The Vietnam War ended and man flew to the moon. I fell in love, and travel did prove to be an education.

Later, I watched in awe as my children's lives took shape. I experienced happiness in situations I never thought that I would: the unconditional love of a child. The joy in helping people.

The Velvet Revolution in Czechoslovakia freed people in my country and I decided to go back to Prague, to see the change. I took my thirteen-year-old daughter with me. I booked us at the same hotel where I had stayed with my mother.

The hotel lobby looked mostly the way I remembered it. There was a couple checking in with a boy who looked to be about eleven. The clerk at the desk was now old and bald. He handed the couple the key to their room. Then he looked at the boy over his spectacles, and said, "What an interesting boy."

My daughter rolled her eyes, recognizing bullshit when she heard it. I smiled at her with satisfaction and pride, humming quietly, "Non, je ne regrette rien."

No Regrets, published by *Burningword Literary Journal*, July 2021

swimmers

The pool at Rutgers University in New Jersey smelled of moisture and chlorine. But on the day of the meet, the overwhelming sense oozing from every fiber of the place was adrenaline and expectations. The pool's facility was large enough to accommodate not only the swimmers but also spectators. Because of its size, the New Jersey Junior Olympics were held there.

I became a qualified US Swimming official, which allowed me to get more involved in my daughter Helena's chosen sport. She had just started high school. It was a bittersweet return to the sport I had an uneasy relationship with.

In Communist Czechoslovakia, where I grew up, everyone was identified by what they did out of school. Runner, piano player, hockey player, singer...

I decided to be a swimmer. I was the only girl on a team of seventeen, though with two brothers to look after me, my mother deemed me protected. But when we started to travel to swim meets, I had nobody to share the hotel room with and I became lonely.

I started to work on my best friend, Magda, (the very same I would use as a cover for my trips to Prague) who had no interest in swimming. It took me a year to convince her. Just before a big meet, Magda, who was not a bad swimmer, still could not dive. I begged the coach to take her with us to the meet.

"I tell you what," said the coach, "if you can teach her to dive by tomorrow, she can come to the meet."

I think Magda learned to dive out of sheer desperation to get me off her back, but I finally had a roommate. At the pool I was very encouraging toward my friend and probably somewhat—a lot, maybe—patronizing. So, I could not believe when I touched the pool's wall, looked Magda's way ready to wait for her, and realized she beat me by a full body length. After that I switched to backstroke and then medley, and then I gave up swimming. Ever my regret.

At seven a.m. I walked to the familiar room at Rutgers where all the officials gathered before the start of every meet. Each official was assigned two lanes to watch for any infractions during the turns.

I watched Helena lose her first race. The hundred-yard breaststroke.

"You had a bad turn at seventy-five yards," I told her. "You'll do better at two hundred tomorrow."

But the next day was no better. Each race, three each day, was a painful disappointment. After the meet, my daughter decided to give up the sport I knew she loved.

The last race of the meet was the 1500-yard freestyle, a twenty-or-so-minute race, depending on the slowest swimmer. There is not much to watch for in freestyle since, as is implied, the swimmer can swim any way they like. I watched the swimmers perform perfect turns and soon my mind started to wander...

Piestany, my hometown in Czechoslovakia, was a powerhouse of swimming, often rivaling much larger cities; however, the real fame for the town and the country came after I left. Martina Moravcova became the most successful swimmer and athlete in Slovakia. She was World Champion twenty-two times, broke three world records, and won two silver medals at the Olympic Games in Sydney. Martina became a friend and a role model to my daughter.

Water played an important role in the town of Piestany, going back two thousand years. Several hot springs originated some 6000 feet under the River Vah, creating hot sulfate–carbonate water, and Piestany became known for its healing hot springs and mud. Many famous people visited the area and some were treated at the spa. The daughter of Czech painter and illustrator Alfonse Mucha was treated at the spa and the grateful artist donated a large painting of his daughter in a wheelchair to the town of Piestany, which led me to a thought.

* * *

"Why are you wearing your official's uniform?" asked Helena, not unreasonably, the following Saturday.

"I am officiating a meet and I need you to help me."

"To do what?" she asked. "If you think I'd go to some stupid meet with you, think again. I'm done with swimming."

Her voice raised in decibels with each word. She'd not gone to practice the whole week.

"This is a very different type of meet," I said.

"I don't care."

"I'll buy you that heart necklace you have been nagging me about," I promised.

"That's blackmail!" she protested.

"I prefer to call it a bribe."

She hesitated, but then asked, "How long will the meet last? There are no finals, I hope?"

"I'll tell you in the car and no, no finals, so we will be back by lunchtime. But we have to hurry now or we will be late."

"You, Mum, will be late, not me," Helena insisted, letting me know she was still uncommitted.

Keeping an eye on the road I explained this was a meet for disabled athletes, which was why I needed her help. She made a face, but when she realized I was pulling into the Rutgers pool, she exploded.

"Well done, Mum. Take me back to the place of my 'triumph,'" she said sarcastically.

"Come on. I am promising you the heart necklace!"

"Hmm." She groaned, and I could tell she was wondering what else she could squeeze out of me. We walked inside the building where she had experienced disappointment, was it only last week?

But the atmosphere in the pool had a different feel. During the warmup the kids in the water appeared not much different than

Martina Moravcova and Helena at meet in Monte Carlo

did Helena and her teammates the week before. But the wheel-chairs and crutches on the deck of the pool said otherwise.

"How do you know when to DQ (disqualify) them?" asked Helena, getting interested.

"I call the infraction same as if you were swimming. The meet referee decides if the disqualification stands or not depending on the severity of the athlete's disability."

"Rather you than me." She shook her head. "I'd feel terrible to DQ those kids."

"They are athletes. Just like you. They worked just as hard as you did to win their medals." Helena knew about disabled athletes in theory but had never met them quite so close up.

"And hurt just as much as you do when they lose," I added.

The national anthem played, signaling the start of the meet. The job of volunteers like Helena was to help with the wheelchairs or crutches before and after each race. She would wheel the chair out of the way once the athlete slipped into the water, or she would hold the crutches until the swimmer needed to lean on them and then take them away. Then reverse the process after the race had finished.

I watched my daughter's athletic body move with ease among the swimmers. With her blonde hair tied into a ponytail, she seemed taller than usual. Her smile revealed her braces as she chatted with one of the girls while she handed her the equipment she was holding for her. I could see she was fully into the competition, but perhaps missing the spirit of the meet.

She watched two girls maneuvering their wheelchairs toward their assigned lanes. Clearly, the girls were best friends. Each girl had a number of scars on her legs, some almost faded away and some quite new and angry-looking.

"Good luck, Hannah," said the first girl and slid into the water in Lane 4. Her friend, Barbara, slid into Lane 5. Middle lanes, designated for top-ranked swimmers. The girls hugged one more time and the race was on.

Hannah led all the way and I could see Helena cheer for her. But at the end, Barbara touched Hannah out for the win.

The week before at JO's, Helena was leading the race in the 400 individual medley. At one point she was half a pool ahead, but she was touched out in the last second by her close friend. So, today I watched for her reaction.

"So unfair!" She came over and whispered in my ear before she fetched the wheelchairs for the two friends still in the water.

Hannah and Barbara were hugging each other and laughing. Helena helped both girls with their wheelchairs. They thanked her and pushed away, excited, recounting the race experience to each other.

For a moment, I wondered if bringing my daughter to the meet was a good idea. I was interrupted by the starter's gun, and I had to focus on the next race.

"Thanks for asking me to come and help," Helena said on the way to the car. I looked into my daughter's blue eyes, searching for sarcasm, but found none.

We drove to the mall and at last my daughter got the heart necklace. She did not quip how she deserved it and I thought she hugged me just a bit longer than usual.

The next day, Sunday, Helena packed her school bag after dinner and before she went to her room, she said as a matter of fact, "Don't forget to put your alarm on for four forty-five a.m."

I looked up.

"That's right," she said. "I'm going to the morning practice."

She turned and went upstairs to her bedroom.

a house with a soul

Most of us have heard about a house with a friendly ghost. Or even an unfriendly one. But the house I am talking about has a soul. The email in front of me confirms it. I lean back in my chair, close my eyes, and take inventory of my memory...

I think it was our second date when my boyfriend told me about his dream to buy a house on Cape Cod. We both lived in London at the time, and I barely knew him. I was not quite sure where exactly Cape Cod was, but since he was from Boston and talked with starry eyes about summers at the Cape, I figured they were geographically related. I nodded more to be polite than out of interest.

I did marry that young man, Jim, and it was not long before his business relocated us to Hong Kong. It seemed the house in Cape Cod would have to wait. But I had barely had time to taste my first dim sum when my husband returned to his favorite subject.

"I don't know how long we will be here or where we will go next, so we ought to have a place we can always come to. A family anchor." He paused, making sure that he had my full attention. "We should buy a house on Cape Cod. It's a perfect place for kids and, while we are in Hong Kong, my parents could keep an eye on the place."

"Ohm." I emitted a muffled response and thought, how could I argue with that?

My husband had hoped for a more enthusiastic reaction, so, to support his case, he added, "I hear the heat and the humidity in July and August here are brutal."

"We've just arrived; I may like the humidity," I said. To me, there was something about Hong Kong that felt magical. I wanted to explore the culture and the mystique that surrounded me.

"Let's visit my parents in Boston this summer and I will show you Cape Cod." He was not giving up. "If you don't like it, we won't buy a house there. Sound fair?"

"Yes, it does," I agreed.

On the drive down Route 3, along the south shore of Massachusetts, my husband's eyes sparkled with excitement. I was groggy from jet lag. Our son Jimmy snored gently, spread on the back seat of my father-in-law's car.

My first impressions of Cape Cod were none too favorable. To a European, the houses looked unexciting. They were all made of wood, covered in gray shingles, and mostly built in the same style. "Have these people not heard of brick or paint?" I thought.

I was not sure if my blood had thinned from the heat in Hong Kong, but for August the air on Cape Cod felt cool. The beach was covered in seaweed and where there was sand, it had grass growing out of it. So far, I was not impressed.

We had pizza for lunch, which proved to be a mistake. Each bite I ate sat in my stomach like the bricks I felt should have been used to build the houses.

We met with a real estate agent. I had it all worked out; after my husband saw all the houses he wanted to see, I would explain that it was not the right place for us. But, I would point out, I had tried.

We turned onto Saquatucket Bluffs Road to see house number four. I liked the name. The house stood on a clearing surrounded by woods. It was gray, yes, but inexplicably, it captured my attention.

I stepped over the threshold into the house's small entry hall. A cranberry-colored, glass light fixture hung from the ceiling, spotlighting our little troupe. The agent opened the door and I stepped into a large, sunny room, followed by my husband and our son.

For a moment I stood in the hall alone. The sun's reflection sent pink sparks in my direction, and I could feel the house welcoming me home. My heart responded instantly.

"This is a double living room, very bright—" The agent started his sales pitch, but I interrupted him.

"We have to buy this house." I looked at Jim with a finality that surprised the agent and shocked my husband.

"Excuse us." He took me outside. "You haven't seen the house yet..."

"I know, but this IS my home. I feel it in my heart. We have to buy this house," I pleaded.

"Okay, but I beg you, don't say another word. I want to negotiate."

"Oh no, no negotiation," I said in panic. "I can't lose this house; this is my home."

We went back to the room where the somewhat-amused agent waited for us. I felt the room opened its heart and welcome us in. Three walls of the room were occupied by a series of windows overlooking, intermittently, a grass lawn and pine trees. On the fourth wall stood a fireplace set in wooden panels. On each side of the fireplace was a door. The door on its left took us into a cozy dining room reminiscent of a sea captain's cabin. A swing door led to a large yellow kitchen dominated by a replica of a wooden table from a whaling ship.

Cape Cod houses, I learned later, got their charm from the way people added to them. Most started as very small summer cottages and, over time, their owners added rooms according to the owner's needs. A new family room bore a painted wooden sign: "Last Addition."

The big bay window overlooked the harbor. Several sailboats were bobbing on their slips as the local fishermen passed by the boats, leaving a wake behind them. A small walkway led into a huge room with two double-sized, four-poster beds that took my breath away. The agent called it the master bedroom.

Needless to say, we bought the house. The owners offered us some of their furniture. We bought that, too.

When we arrived at the Saquatucket house the next summer, there were four of us. Our second son, Danny, had been born in Hong Kong that spring. For the next thirty years, the house watched us grow and grow up. We built a large pool so that I could swim laps, since I never quite reconciled with the beach. The pool proved to be the pulse of the house.

No matter where we lived in the winter, we would spend the summer in our house on Cape Cod. My husband was right; the house was our anchor. Eventually we stopped roaming around the world and settled in New Jersey, where our daughter, Helena, was born. For the next twenty years we traveled the five-plus hours from New Jersey so that we could spend the whole summer in our little gray paradise. I learned to like the gray houses, I accepted the seaweed on the beach, and soon pizza encountered a thin crust.

Jim, who worked in New York, commuted cheerfully every weekend so that he could spend it with us on Cape Cod. I decorated and redecorated the house according to the changing ages of the children. The house did not mind. I never touched its bones, and in return, the house protected us. During Hurricane Bob, in 1991, we lost eleven trees but not a single window.

Sailing became a passion for our older boy, Jimmy. He joined the local sailing club and became a very competent sailor. He convinced his father to buy a catboat and taught him to sail it. My husband fell under the spell of sails and wind.

Unlike the tide that goes in and out every six hours without much change, every summer when we arrived, the children were taller.

During high school and college, the boys found summer jobs on Cape Cod. They invited their friends and created their own traditions. The Fourth of July was reserved for my oldest and his friends. Their nights were spent locked in fearsome games of Scrabble. The next morning, I would find dictionaries and score papers scattered all over the porch, where most of the battles took place.

Labor Day belonged to my younger son Danny and his friends. Some years there would be seven, even eight boys staying with us. Their Labor Day baseball games were famous. The house had a front seat to some fine matches as well as some embarrassing performances. The achievements got bigger and better with each retelling.

Those games were "huge." Just ask any of the boys. Given their baseball skills, a spectator would not have guessed that there was a future professor at Tulane University, Hillary Clinton's chief speech writer, and Antonin Scalia's Supreme Court clerk among them. The boys are now men and they are all very successful, still best friends and still poor baseball players.

When Helena left for college and we became empty-nesters, I insisted that we move to New York City. I called it my midlife crisis. My husband had one eye on retirement and the other on buying a boat. HE decided to sell our Cape Cod home and buy a house with a dock.

The boys, who by now were in San Francisco and Chicago, respectively, were shocked that he would even think about selling the Saquatucket house. How could he do that? As they protested, I thought about the house in New Jersey where they grew up. When we sold it after twenty years, the boys, who were away in grad school, did not even bother to come and see it for the last time before we moved out.

But the Cape Cod house was different. It was where all their treasures and memories resided. Where they met with their summer friends, where they dreamed and matured. I recognized that glazed, starry look in their eyes. I had seen it many years earlier. I did not understand it then; this time, I did.

My daughter embraced the new house first. She was always ready for something new. Jimmy was the next to give up the fight. The sight of all the boats in the harbor, looking toward Nantucket, ready to sail, broke down our older son's resistance. Vindicating the reputation of middle children everywhere, Danny proved to be most difficult to sway. When we finally convinced him to see the new house, he dug his heels in even firmer.

"There's no baseball field here," he announced, referring to the patch of grass in front of the other house, *his* house. He was right. The land did slope rather steeply toward the water and the dock.

"I know," I said, trying to be sympathetic. "The baseball games are a tradition."

"Epic, Mum, epic," he corrected me.

At first, the challenge of finding the right owner for the Saquatucket house was not evident. In fact, we thought we had the house sold the very first month it was on the market. The inspection went well, but at the last minute, the sale fell through. Then we had two separate people at the same time bidding for the house. We accepted one of them, but again the sale fell through. We contacted the other, who reconfirmed his offer, but...ditto. We rented out the house for the summer, hoping that someone would fall in love with it during their stay. Again, there were several near-misses. In my heart I came to believe that the house rejected them.

I admit I did not like them either and I was relieved each time these would-be buyers disappeared. Naturally, I did not share this bit of wisdom with anyone.

We settled in the new house. One gloomy day toward the end of the fourth summer of renting the Saquatucket house, I missed it more than usual. I drove over and as I walked in, I felt an overwhelming sadness. I sat on the back stairs and cried. I looked out the window. It started to rain. The windows, like my cheeks, were wet. And so, for a while, the house and I cried together.

Slowly, I started to remember the happy days, and as my tears began to dry, I could see it all so clearly. The day we arrived from Hong Kong. Our new baby boy in a wicker basket decorated in

Laura Ashley fabric. Teaching all the children to swim in our over-sized pool. The Superman and Batman capes flying behind running little boys. Arriving from New Jersey for the summer and finding our neighbor's boy, Brian, waiting for us at the door. The group of kids playing an invented game in the dirt behind the house. The boys getting covered in poison ivy after playing manhunt in the dark. The joy of a Red Sox win, and the disappointment of a loss. My father-in-law taking the boys fishing and my mother-in-law telling me how tea was the best meal of the day. Brian sticking a fishing hook in his own head while attempting to cast his fishing line. The "Marco Polo" games in the pool that drove our neighbors to early cocktails.

The highlight of the summer was always the fight for the captaincy. All the boys in the neighborhood vied for control of an inflated boat in the pool with my brother Jan, who visited every year from Washington, DC. The boys tried to tear him down from his perch on the float. He would taunt them, singing, "It's nice to be a captain."

When we bought the house, we were told that the owner's mother-in-law lived downstairs, in what the agent called the master bedroom, to save her going up the stairs. For us, the room instantly became the mother-in-law suite. My father-in-law did not mind. After they both passed away, we never moved into the room. For us it was always the mother-in-law suite.

It was the largest room in the house, converted from a two-car-garage. There were two four-poster double beds with a massive dresser between them. Another huge old dresser with an attached mirror stood opposite. The children would play many exciting games on rainy afternoons in there. And when guests came to visit, they would gasp at the size of the room and at the idea that it was allocated to them.

Now I walked into the mother-in-law suite and sat on one of the four-poster beds. The rain started to subside. I stretched out on the bed and marveled at how little the room had changed over the years. I thought of that day almost thirty years ago, when I almost gave my husband a heart attack after I declared the house to be our home while standing in the front hallway.

I got thirsty, so I went to the kitchen to get a glass of water. Looking at the tiles on the backsplash, I had to laugh. I remembered the year when I had the kitchen remodeled. The tiles featured the local fish. Cod, sole, snapper, and the mighty humpback. The kitchen looked like it belonged to a fishmonger. You had to be a Cape Codder to love it.

Suddenly, I could hear a baby cry. I ran upstairs to our bedroom. The familiar room seemed to smile at me. Every tiny piece of that room had a memory attached to it. Each of the children started their Cape Cod life in this room before they moved to their respective bedrooms. It felt so very familiar.

Just then, I heard a boy's laughter. I walked to the room we called the boys' dormitory. There were times when the two pullout, trundle beds would house as many as eight boys. Head to toe, they called it. Now it was empty.

Suddenly, the house was very quiet. I could hear its breath, or was it mine? For a while, we breathed in unison. It was a powerful feeling. Was it goodbye? I passed my daughter's room and noticed that the picture made out of the little characters spelling her name, H-e-l-e-n-a, still hung on the wall above the bed. My friend Jillian, an artist, gave it to me on Helena's first birthday.

I locked the house and stepped into blinding sunshine. I kept the whole experience to myself, ever my own treasure.

That fall, back in our New York apartment, my husband and I were having breakfast when his phone rang.

"Hello," he said. At first, I continued to eat my eggs. But soon the half-conversation got my attention.

"Aha...Yes...Yes, I shall talk to my wife...I don't think that would be a problem...Absolutely...Yes, I'll call you back after I speak with my wife...Yes, today."

I put down my toast. "The young couple saw the house yesterday, liked it, and made an offer," Jim said.

"Go on."

"They want to buy the furniture as well."

"Tell me about the couple," I said, and thought about the boy's laughter and an infant's cry the last time I was in the Saquatucket house. "Do they have children?" I asked, my pulse quickening.

"No, they got married recently. They live in California, but he's from Massachusetts and she's from Maryland. They want a place close to their families. They love the house as is."

I liked them already.

"Not much of a negotiation," mused my husband. "It reminds me of when we bought the house." I opened my mouth but thought it was wiser to close it silently.

The young couple bought the house. I was at peace. I knew that the house had found the right couple to replace us.

When we met the new owners, we felt as if we knew them. Tom and Monica met at a friend's wedding in Italy. They fell in love and got married after a whirlwind romance. They were keeping the mother-in-law suite as a mother-in-law suite, both having living parents. By their first summer, they had a baby boy with an infectious laugh, and I learned that Monica makes the world's best peach cobbler.

By their third summer, they were expecting a daughter.

I open my eyes and I am almost surprised to find myself in New York. The memory of the past can be powerful. But it is the present that makes it lasting. I read the email one more time. "You will be pleased to know, that there will be a Helena at the Saquatucket house again."

It was signed, "TOM AND MONICA."

There is a Supreme Court clerk and Hillary Clinton chief speech writer in that group

the blackboard

The fear of elastic-waist pants lurked at the back of my mind for a long time. Though the frequency increased about the time when the cleaners began to "shrink" my pants, especially in the waist.

My daughter and I "officially" became the same size after she graduated from college and needed to borrow a suit for a job interview. My black suit did very nicely, thank you. Before the job interview, my daughter viewed my closet as one of a sensible (read *old,)* lady, containing clothes she would never wear. After the job interview, (which resulted in her first job), my wardrobe was upgraded, in her mind, to "classic."

Growing up with two older brothers in a country where clothing was passed down from the oldest to the youngest regardless of gender, I was used to wearing pants and shirts. The vest was worn for warmth and storage: holding keys, hankies, and

American chewing gum in its numerous pockets. I was sporting the *Annie Hall* look minus the tie, long time before the movie was written. After I had seen the movie, by which time I was living in London, I adopted the tie with glee. Once I could afford it, I bought my ties at Liberty of London. The miniature flowers on the fabric were in hues that reminded me of the springs, summers, and autumns in Czechoslovakia when I was a child. The cotton was so fine that a less knowledgeable person could be forgiven for mistaking the delicate fabric for silk.

After the Soviets crushed The Prague Spring, wearing "Liberty," as it were, around my neck, gave me a satisfaction that was perhaps missed by some. I fancied Annie Hall would get it. Dresses made only guest appearances in my wardrobe.

My mother always wore dresses. So, as any self-respecting teenager would, I rebelled against dresses and eyed them with suspicion. I never put on a frock until I became a model and was paid to do so. Now, in a role reversal, my daughter suggested I "upgrade" my wardrobe with some dresses.

Verbal shorthand developed between my daughter and me when shopping together. If she told me I looked "really cool" in a dress, it meant the following: she wanted it, could not afford it, and hoped I would buy it so she could borrow it. I usually followed the protocol; the agreement earned me the key to my daughter's apartment so I could retrieve the wandering garments should I have use for them. That is not to say that some of my daughter's garments have not made an appearance in my closet. But that was fine. She never did give us her key back.

Clothing was always a big part of my life. My father, a tailor, told me that clothing made a person, but a person made clothing.

"Be your own tailor," he advised.

I put on a pair of borderline-stretchy jeans, a crisp white shirt, one of my Liberty ties, and my favorite vest.

I caught my reflection in the mirror; dressed in my writer's attire, I was ready to poke the long sleeping bear. I listen to the debate in my head:

You want to become a writer at the age of sixty? said my sensible self.

Why not? said the cool-dressed person.

You tried it before. Besides, nobody wants to hear what an old lady has to say.

Ruth Bader Ginsburg became a Supreme Court Justice at the age of sixty. And she became the Notorious RBG at the age of eighty-two.

You can't spell.

True...True, spelling is tricky. But I can go to school.

You'll be a granny to your fellow students...

My inner monologues evaporated when my daughter walked into my bedroom, a key and shopping bag in hand.

"J. Crew had a sale," she announced. "I bought new pants we can share."

As she slowly unwrapped the pants, the gentle swish of soft tissue paper had my full attention. I did not notice the sly look on my daughter's face. When she finished unwrapping, she held up the pants, placing them first against her hips, and then mine. I looked horrified at their elastic waist.

"Put them on, Mum," she said. "Face your fears."

* * *

And so I did. I enrolled in a school for continuing education at NYU. I settled on a creative nonfiction class.

For my first class I arrived thirty minutes early. I found walking the corridors of the school at once scary and exhilarating. Would I be the oldest? Would I be the only person with an accent? Would my writing be interesting enough?

I carried a bag containing my computer, a spiral-bound notebook, and several pens. (In case I would run out of ink?) I was eyeing the door where my class was going to be held and I waited for people to enter. Feeling like a teenager, I did not want to be the geek who was always first in the class. The class started at six p.m. and we were supposed to come fifteen minutes early.

I looked at my watch. It was five forty-five and the classroom was empty. I started to move toward the door when from the opposite side of the corridor a cluster of about five people came and entered the classroom. I sighed in relief. The people who entered the room were young, but definitely not teenagers.

I walked in right behind them and sat behind the closest desk to the door. In an effort to fit in, I slouched exactly the way I used to tell my children not to slouch when they were young. I opened my notebook and pretended to write while doodling houses, a pressure release since the time when I really was a teen. I felt the adrenaline rush through me and almost giggled.

Just then, the teacher walked in. We knew she was not a student even before she sat at the teacher's desk. She had a confident stride and looked at us directly.

"My name is Connie and I am your teacher." She told us a bit about herself while I checked her out. She was about my age. I sensed some leftover Flower Power in her appearance, which made me like her. Although she was a teacher, I could tell that she was principally a writer and an artist.

Our class was diverse in age, gender, and in nationality. The ages ranged from eighteen to early sixties. I could not be sure about my fellow students' ages, as nobody announced it. There were two students, one male and one female, who looked to be my age.

Connie asked us to introduce ourselves and give an abbreviated bio of ourselves. I learned that the male student, who looked only a little younger than I, was British, an early retiree with a thirst to see the world and the desire to write about it. With the typical English sensibility, he was taking a writing course. The female student was German, living in New York, and to my delight had a real accent. There was also a teenager from Denmark, full of idealistic resolve but with a limited grip on the English language. He was me at his age. There was a brooding young man from Belarus with a wicked sense of humor, and a sweet young woman from Korea. The rest of the students were Americans of different ages.

* * *

I watched the first snowflakes of winter starting to cover up the pavements. The roads were still dark, the traffic dissipating the fragile pieces of lace falling from the sky. As much as I favored fall, there was something special about the first snow of winter.

I was early again for my class. It would be our last in the course. This time when I walked into the classroom, the teacher was already in the room and on the blackboard she wrote:

Write,
Write every day,
Write all the time.
Write in your journal,

Write stories that may not connect, but keep writing.

I wish I had known that when I put my notebook out of reach after the night of disappointment.

I believe I am entitled to one cliché in the book: "It is never too late."

apples and oranges

Autumn in New York was my favorite time to be in the city. The sun was cool, but the wind was gentle and surprisingly warm, creating a fluffy protection against the October air. Walking home with my provisions for lunch, I felt the excitement build inside me. Not just because I was becoming a senior citizen, but also because I was going to share the day with my old boss.

In the morning I had put on my favorite jeans and white shirt. I tied my bright Versace tie loosely around my neck, pulling it side to side a few times to get the desired "chill" look. I looked in the mirror and decided I needed to put on my vest to give my body some shape and to protect the tie while cooking.

I remembered Erin liked scallops. I lightly sautéed onions, garlic, tomatoes, and freshly grated turmeric root, which turned my saucepan into Van Gogh's gold-and-red fields of Provençale.

I put in the scallops and they quickly absorbed the tangy flavor of the herbs and filled the kitchen air with the lightness of ocean mist with a hint of exotic promise. I sprinkled the finely chopped rich green leaves of tarragon and they turned the whole dish into spring in autumn. The dish reflected how I felt.

The doorbell rang. Excited, I threw the door open. There she was, petite, still beautiful, dressed in a classic navy-blue pants suit. She looked much younger than her passport would have us believe. She held a bouquet of sunflowers in her hand, my favorite. She, too, remembered. We hugged to a chorus of happy screams.

"What, no apple and an orange to keep up my vitamin supply?" I joked, reminding Erin of the many inspections I had to go through before I was allowed to start work at the London Playboy Club, where Erin was my supervisor, too many years ago...

Up to the sixth floor, to the Bunny Mother's office I would go.

Hair styled? Check.

Nails groomed and painted? Check.

Shoe color matching the color of my silk costume? Check.

Two pairs of tights? Check.

A little twirl for Bunny Mother's eyes concluded the inspection. From the big box next to her desk I picked up an apple and an orange to help me ward off germs, and I was sent to my assigned work for the night.

There were four restaurants, a discotheque, and a casino at the Playboy building on London's Park Lane. Playboy was a members-only club and very popular with American visitors. A piece of home, perhaps, that offered a decent steak and French fries, not to mention full bottles of ketchup and mustard in the middle of the table, unheard of in London at that time. The Playmate Bar was on the ground floor. The name was derived from the wall behind the bar that hosted pictures of Playboy centerfolds.

The next three floors were a mix of restaurants and casinos. On a landing just before the top floor, which was casino only, was a gift shop where I liked to work. It was working in the gift shop that earned me the "Top Bunny" distinction. Apparently, I was a natural salesperson. The other reason I liked to work in the gift shop was that it required almost no walking.

Given that I had put in a day's work already, I was glad to save my feet. Both my day and night jobs required me to wear high heels. This was long before sneakers on the street were acceptable and even longer before the ballet shoe made its appearance. So, whether I was going on auditions for a modeling or acting job, or working in a photo studio or TV set, unless the costume dictated otherwise, I had to wear high-heeled shoes.

Modeling was a job that provided for few long-term friendships, but in the Playboy Club, I would see familiar faces every time I came to work. The girls may have worked on different floors, but you saw them in the "Bunny Room," where we changed and put on our makeup. There was a hair stylist on duty for the girls who needed help.

Adjacent to the Bunny Room was a lounge where we could watch television or munch on the aforementioned apple or an orange.

There was plenty for women's lib to pick on, no doubt, but at that time of my life, working at the club helped me immensely and I knew I possessed the ultimate defense. The little word NO. And if that did not work, I could draw on my childhood. Having grown up with two older brothers in the neighborhood where

I was an only girl among a gang of fifteen or so boys, I knew how to aim and hit the balls, and not just the plastic ones.

At Playboy I met girls who, like me, had long-term plans, and working at the club helped them to achieve their goals. We had girls who studied at the London School of Economics; we had dancers, actresses, musicians, or those just saving up for a mortgage. We even had an equestrian.

* * *

I poured a chilled glass of wine and recounted to Erin how my daughter could not believe that we had to wear two pairs of tights.

"What? Two pairs of tights?" She'd rolled her eyes in disbelief.

"Oh yes, no leg skin could be seen," laughed Erin. "No smoking, no drinking, no dating customers and two pair of tights!"

"Young girls today would think we were working in a convent," I said.

"To the nun and the Mother Superior!" We clinked our glasses.

I had stayed in close contact with Erin's sisters, Tricia and Carmel, with whom I lived during a very difficult time of my life, as described earlier, when I needed protection from an aggressive boyfriend. Tricia and Carmel not only stood by me; they protected me.

When Tricia wrote to me that Erin was going to be in New York, naturally, I was thrilled. It was a bonus that our meeting fell on my birthday.

While we nursed our wine, we remembered our friends, a "where are they now" kind of inventory, which brought us to Carmel again.

"Dear Carmel. I miss her so much."

"She was one of a kind," said Erin.

Carmel was a beautiful young woman who came to London from Australia with her older sister, Erin, and younger sister, Tricia. All three girls got jobs at the Playboy Club. Shortly after I came to the club, Erin got promoted to the "Bunny Mother."

When I was in dire need, Carmel offered for me to stay with her and Tricia because she too was in England without her family, but there were three of them, and I was alone. Her generosity made it possible for me to save up and buy my own apartment, the first home since I left Czechoslovakia as a wide-eyed eighteen-year-old. Generosity I would never forget!

When I heard that Carmel was sick, I called her in Australia. I miscounted the time zones and I woke her up at five a.m.

"How are you, darling? Hope all is well with you and your family," she said.

It never occurred to her to mention that it was an ungodly hour for me to call her. Happy to hear from me, she wanted to know all about my family, and only after she gave me news about her family did she say, "Excuse me, darling, my voice is a bit raspy from the chemo I am taking. It is a bit of a nuisance, but I am sure it will pass."

I wanted to believe that it was just a bit of a nuisance, and that it was going to pass. But when, a few months later, I received a letter from Tricia, I held it in my hands while my eyes filled with tears, making the letters on the envelope go in and out of focus. I kept staring at the letter as if by keeping it sealed, I could extend Carmel's life.

"Do you remember how Carmel loved the parties we had?" Erin noticed the tears in my eyes, and changed the subject.

Carmel and I in London

Once a year, on Sunday night, the London Playboy Club closed its doors in order to have a party for all the employees. It was an open bar and free food for all. None of the top bosses came, so that everybody could relax and have fun. We all put on our best frocks. For the girls, the night was a fashion parade with plenty of individualism mixed in. You could see famous fashion designers Ossie Clarke and Vivienne Westwood, with a few Biba outfits molded into a particular girl's imagination. The guys cared more about comfort, yet somehow kept it chic. We got to know the room directors socially, and we joked with bartenders who could get testy on busy nights if a girl messed up the drink orders. We had a chance to see them in a different light.

The gay guys were the best dressed. One of the more flamboyant bartenders, Frank, always called me Zsa-Zsa. He insisted I looked like Zsa-Zsa Gabor. Frank, who claimed to have met Miss Gabor, insisted that it was more than my accent. I had heard of the actress, but I had no idea what she looked like, so I took his word for it.

On the dance floor, one could see a lot of talent. We had dancers who appeared on different theater stages all over London. We even had a dancer who performed in Paris. My friend Emma, who trained with me, danced in Covent Garden in the revival of *Carmen*. All this talent made me feel sorely inadequate as a dancer, but I knew I was among friends. Nobody was judging me, and I would dance the night away.

"Yes, the parties were fun," I agreed, "but my favorite memories are the memories of promotions."

"You were my favorite person to send on promotions," said Erin.

* * *

Most of the promotions were for a charitable cause, but there were a few that were not. I recalled a photoshoot in Germany for Jägermeister. And then there was the trip to Milan, where I wandered off and almost did not make it back to the hotel to catch the flight back. But most of all, I was proud of our visits to London's Great Ormond Street Hospital for children.

During the holidays we used to bring toys, books, and games for the children who were being treated at the hospital. There was a special ensemble for those trips: black turtleneck sweaters, black opaque tights, and short white skirts. We did wear our bunny ears, which must have seemed strange to the children, most of whom had never heard of the Playboy Club and certainly had never been inside one.

I did not think the children really cared who we were; we brought toys and diverted their attention from the treatment they had to endure. The children's faces would light up, and for a brief moment, they could forget where they were and why. After each visit, I felt I was not just a waitress in high heels and an uncomfortable costume. I was proud to have a job that also included spreading kindness and giving much-needed distraction to those who suffered.

Erin offered to help me wash the dishes. I handed her a plastic apron and a dishcloth. Two women looking as if they had stepped out of a fashion magazine, yet wearing rubber gloves and plastic aprons, no doubt made quite a surreal picture.

"What are your plans, Erin?" I asked.

"Well, I don't plan to stay at home and knit," she quipped.

"It would be a very long scarf." I laughed.

"I might go to school, learn about computers. I don't want to be dependent on my daughter's free time. What about you?"

"Actually, I am taking a course on writing. Perhaps I will retrieve my old dream to be a writer."

Erin watched me wipe the kitchen counter over and over.

"You have plenty of role models," she said.

Images of former bunnies inserted themselves in my mind. Debbie Harry, Susan Sullivan, Lauren Hutton, and yes, arguably, even Gloria Steinem, who owes her break into journalism to her well-written exposé about the Chicago Playboy Club.

I didn't see myself fit into that category. Then I thought about Carmel and all the girls who were not fortunate enough to get old. I owed it to them not to squander my time on doubt and fear. And since when did I give in to fear?

"Perhaps I will write about our lunch," I said.

Erin pointed at apples and oranges in my fruit basket (some habits die hard). "Why not? Life is full of apples and oranges."

free spirits

A few weeks into my husband's retirement, I was leafing through magazines looking for a clue where to park the energy that was circulating in our veins when Jim came into the room. He watched me tapping the keys on my computer.

"What are you doing?" he asked.

"Writing." I did not want to tell Jim about the thought that kept wandering into my mind. Nobody would invite a witness to a possible failure.

"What are you writing?"

"Just an email," I lied.

"Who to?"

"My brother. It can wait." I closed the computer. "Would you like some tea?"

"Oh, not sure. I just had coffee. Maybe later." He continued to linger in the kitchen.

How hard could it be to decide if you wanted tea or coffee, and if you want it now or later? I thought. Maybe if I started to wash dishes, he would leave. It always worked before.

"You should soak the pots first before you wash them," came some advice.

"Thanks for the tip; I didn't know that," I said, but Jim missed the sarcasm.

"You're welcome," he said.

I had struck out again. While my fingers itched to open the computer, Jim decided to have a boiled egg.

"I'll make it for you." I jumped at the opportunity to get him out of my kitchen.

"Thank you, but you've been doing most of the cooking up till now; I can do it."

Most? I raised my eyebrow but stayed silent.

Like a Boy Scout who comes home from his first weekend outing and wants to show off his newly gained knowledge, my dear husband suddenly felt the need to educate me in the art of boiling an egg.

I pointed out that I had hard-boiled eggs before.

"It was a suggestion."

Damn. Now I had done it. He meant well, I told myself. I looked at my closed computer, and was about to segue elsewhere when he did it for me. Onto a subject I was hoping to avoid, sailing.

This was not exactly a new passion. The interest in sailing took hold through our oldest son, who had become an enthusiast, eventually showing his father how to sail, and introduced the notion of owning a boat. Enter the Free Spirit, a thirty-four-foot Bristol built the year my daughter, now finishing college, was born.

I come from a landlocked country and he wanted me to be a sailor, but I was ready to make a pact with Poseidon if it meant I would be able to sit in my kitchen and explore my idea without interruption. I agreed to take part in the sailing school.

A youthful-looking Boomer retiree welcomed our small class with infectious enthusiasm, but I soon discovered that I had very little interest in prevailing winds and similar nautical data. The practice was even worse. Being an indecisive person by nature, I felt exponentially more unsure given the knowledge that my decision could capsize the boat.

Jim, on the other hand, was soaking it all up. At the conclusion of the school, we all had to take a test. My husband scored the highest in the class, and I the lowest. I took comfort in the thought that we averaged somewhere in the middle.

Free Spirit was an excellent boat with lots of wood, the hull painted navy blue with gold trim and white sails. She had a center cockpit with manual mainsail and a jib in the front. The main cabin was aft on the boat and connected to one of the two showers and heads.

Forward was the V berth and the second shower and head/toilet. On the port side was the navigation station, and on the starboard side was the kitchen, or in nautical terms, the "galley."

One of the things that legitimized our boat as a serious sailing vessel was that our cooker was gimbaled. I pictured myself "calmly" cooking goulash on the perfectly gimbaled, always level cooker while high winds tossed the boat about.

As newly certified sailors, we decided to go to the Elizabeth Islands for our maiden voyage, and we invited our longtime friends Philip and Katrina.

"It'll be an adventure," I told my friends, given that we were too old for midlife crises.

Philip was British, an ex-RAF pilot, and an accomplished sailor. Katrina was possibly the only person in the world who knew less about sailing than I did. My only saving grace was that I could follow directions, which translated to manual work, like winching.

On a clear, sunny morning, Free Spirit sat proudly on her temporary mooring surrounded by hundreds of sailboats in picturesque Sippican Harbor, situated in the heart of Marion. The small New England town relies on Buzzards Bay's waters, both for fishing and for the summer tourist industry. Recreational sailing is a major seasonal activity for residents and visitors alike.

We arrived laden with provisions that would have sufficed for a trip to England. The late August weather was warm, and the harbor looked as if the night sky dropped all its stars on the gently swaying water. The launch took us to our boat, where, with embarrassing clumsiness, we managed to get ourselves and the provisions on board.

In high spirits and full of confidence, we sailed through Buzzards Bay and headed for the Elizabeth Islands and Cuttyhunk. New England's waters do not warm up until the end of the summer, which made our timing perfect. Our menfolk were showing off their sailing knowledge to each other while Katrina and I soaked up the sun.

We reached open water, and the wind became cool but not unpleasant. Suddenly, I understood the magic that people talk about when they speak about sailing. I listened to the sound of the wind and water working in unison, propelling the boat forward between the green-gray water and gray-blue sky.

Katrina is one of my oldest friends. Despite her complete

lack of sailing knowledge, she was the most appropriate person to come with us on this trip. She defies age and can adapt to any conditions. I watched the wind create waves on her cream silk blouse, matching the waves on the ocean. Convention does not apply to my friend. I was sure she would have worn a silk blouse if we were traveling through the jungle.

We planned to drop anchor at Cuttyhunk, the largest of the Elizabeth Islands. There were only a handful of people living on the island, and they lived on their boats.

Philip was first to spot the islands. When we reached the harbor, several boats of different sizes were already bobbing in the relatively shallow waters. We dropped our anchor and cheered as if we had just won America's Cup.

Philip and I jumped off the boat to celebrate with a swim. The water was invigorating and a story about our voyage began to form in my head. When we got back on board, Jim had the grill going, and Katrina had the boat decorated for our first dinner on board, including nautical napkins and dinnerware. We were going to dine in style. I knew there was no other way with Katrina on board.

Philip opened the bottle of champagne we brought with us to christen the boat. Sipping the bubbly, we watched a small motorboat going from sailboat to sailboat. When it stopped by us, we learned that it was a local fisherman selling oysters and mussels. We said no to the mussels, but we loaded up on oysters.

For a few dollars more, the man offered to open the oysters for us. I watched him standing on the rocking boat, expertly manipulating a sharp knife.

Meanwhile, my husband turned hamburgers on the small grill attached to the aft of the boat. Katrina made a fresh salad from the provisions we brought with us. The meal was a feast, and after we finished eating, we marveled at our good fortune the weather had afforded us. Since I hadn't done anything all day, I took on the cleaning duty.

With everything shipshape, we relaxed under the sky already in our comfortable night outfits. Nursing my drink and feeling very satisfied, I closed my eyes. At that moment, I was pleased we'd bought the boat. I drifted into a salty vacuum, rocked gently by the boat...

And was thrust back into reality by one of the guys pushing me out of the way and telling me to go below. The two men were rushing about, and none answered me when I asked where was Katrina.

I heard a thunderclap, and a moment after the men came below, I could hear torrential rain bouncing off our Bimini. The guys poured themselves a glass of cognac as a reward for managing to batten down all the hatches before the storm hit us.

Just as they clinked their glasses, the boat hit something.

"What was that?" I asked.

"Nothing," the men said, but then there it was once more. Philip put down the drink and ran from the main cabin up to the cockpit. Almost instantly, he called down in his British accent, which was in danger of losing its cool:

"James, we are dragging, and we are bumping against our neighbor. Pass me the steering wheel."

For us to open the table in the cockpit, we had taken down the steering wheel.

"Must be up there," said my husband, pushing me away. The two men ran all over the boat, looking for a very large wheel in a very small space.

So, this is what panic looks like? I thought, and I decided to get out of the way and into our stateroom. I opened the door and there, in clear view on top of the bed, was the wheel. I took the wheel and brought it up to the two stricken men. Further danger was averted, and we all slept in peace for the rest of the night.

I was up first the next morning. I climbed the ladder into the cockpit, dressed in sweatpants and a hoodie, a throwback attire from my youth. I rolled up the clear plastic on the Bimini, which kept us dry from the unexpected rain last night.

I sat in the cockpit and watched the darkness dilute into the color of the chamomile tea my mother used to make for me when I was a child. With each minute, my mother's invisible hand put more lemon into the tea, making it clearer, until I could see the first rays of the sun peeking from the horizon.

The condensation that had accumulated during the night on the boat's deck glimmered in the early rays. The gentle splashing of the water against the side of the boats anchored in the harbor provided a background symphony for the rising of the sun. It was the only sound in the harbor other than the beat of my heart. For that moment, just before the sun or anyone else came up, I had a sense of clarity that was spiritual.

The men came up, clutching hot coffee in their hands.

"Oh, good morning, my wonderful friends." Katrina was standing at the bottom of the ladder and inquired if we wanted anything from the kitchen below before she joined us.

"Did you all sleep well?" she asked. Without waiting for an answer, she continued, "I slept like a rock. It was so peaceful, not a sound."

We looked at each other, grinning.

"Did you hear any noise last night?" asked Philip.

"No, not a sound. Why, did something happen?"

"Well," I said, "first it rained, then we dragged, and the guys couldn't find the steering wheel."

"Oh, why didn't you wake me up? I moved it," she said. "It didn't look good where the guys put it."

The two men stared at her in disbelief.

"You know," Jim said, "everything on the boat has a function..."

"All's well that ends well," I said.

By the time the sun was fully upon us, we had lifted the anchor and sailed toward Martha's Vineyard.

The rest of the trip was uneventful, and we came back to Marion just as the weather turned cool.

Back in my kitchen, I was once again not alone, and receiving suggestions from my bored husband.

Finally, I said, "Look, I married you for better or worse, but not for lunch."

After that, Jim pointedly avoided the kitchen, read the paper, and went out, presumably to meet with friends. A few times he went out for lunch wearing his suit.

Just as my guilt reached an all-time high, he walked in with a bottle of wine.

"What are we celebrating?" I asked.

"You booting me out...and my new job."

a passing fancy

When my daughter was a sophomore in college, I suddenly found myself to be the coolest mom among her friends in the dorm. This was because while she and her pals were tossing around ideas about costumes for Halloween, she mentioned that I'd once worked as a bunny at the London Playboy Club. And I still had a couple of the costumes in my closet. Ears, tail, cuffs and cufflinks, collar and the dickie, all clean in a box and ready to wear. She noticed the envy on her roommates' faces and instantly claimed one of the costumes for herself.

There have seldom been reasons for me to talk about my job at the club, which I have always viewed as being a waitress in an uncomfortable costume and ridiculously high heels. As the girls showered me with questions, my mind flashed back to one particular incident...

Many Americans came to the Playboy Club to get a scotch served with more than one piece of ice, a cold beer, or a Coca-Cola, and possibly the only proper American hamburger in London. I don't know if that was what brought Dustin Hoffman to the club, but I don't think he was there to gamble. He was in London to shoot a movie about the ten lost days of Agatha Christie. It was taking longer than planned and so he came to Playboy several times.

I was working in the gift shop one evening and had no customers when I saw him coming up the stairs toward me. I don't remember my exact words, but they were something like, "Excuse me, have you ever heard of Le Pétomane?"

My boyfriend at the time was hoping to produce a movie about Joseph Pujol, the famous Flatulent Frenchman. I was so engrossed in helping to get the movie off the ground, it seemed perfectly natural to me to ask about an obscure artist as if I were talking about Christie herself.

Pujol came to fame around 1890. He had the rather unique ability to suck in water or air through his rectum. By controlling his abdominal muscles, he learned to create sounds coming out of his nether region. He learned to play music in that manner— perhaps a "passing fancy," if one were to get pun-y—and performed in small theaters, eventually becoming famous enough to perform at Moulin Rouge under the stage name *Le Pétomane*.

"How do YOU know about him?" Hoffman asked. I explained we had an outline for a movie and wondered if he would be interested in playing the lead role.

"I have something on tomorrow," he told me, "but bring it to me at the Hilton the day after tomorrow after five." A group of tourists descended on the gift shop and cut our conversation short, so he wrote down his room number and I told him I'd be there.

I arrived with the pages of the outline and a book about Pujol. When I knocked on his hotel room door, a man came out and told me Mr. Hoffman was in bed and the doctor was with him.

"Ask her to come here." I heard a voice, a bit scratchy but decidedly belonging to Dustin Hoffman. He was in the bed and talking to the doctor.

"Please sit down," he said to me, then to the doctor, "Give me a few minutes; she doesn't bite."

He smiled first at the doctor, then at me. The doctor left and Hoffman listened to my sales pitch, then asked a few more questions about the project and then the usual: where was I from— my accent being obvious. I told him I was from Czechoslovakia and he asked me if I knew Milos Forman. I told him I knew of Forman but I did not know him personally, and I made a mental note to suggest Forman as a director for the movie.

We chatted for a while about the possibilities, and just as the doctor was about to boot me out, Hoffman invited me to a private screening of his new movie, *Straight Time*. He promised he would read the movie outline and we would talk some more after the screening. He said he would call me with the details at the end of the following week.

At the time I was also modeling, and I had a booking to shoot a TV commercial in Germany, but I should have been back in London before the appointed time for the call. Unfortunately, the job was weather sensitive, and the weather did not cooperate and the filming ran over. By the time I got back, it was way too late. I don't know if Dustin Hoffman ever called me because we lived in a time of no answering machines. The next day I learned from the papers that he'd left London for LA.

Many years later, by which time I lived in America, I saw Hoffman walking toward me one day on 57th Street in New York. He was alone and I wondered if I should stop him and remind him of our conversation in London. But I just smiled and let him pass by me. He would not remember anyway, I told myself.

As for *A Passing Fancy,* the idea and I parted company when the boyfriend and I did the same. The Le Pétomane story remains obscure, but Mel Brooks did choose to have some fun with it, naming his somewhat-gaseous character in *Blazing Saddles* Governor Le Pétomane.

* * *

"Mum." My daughter was shaking my arm. "Why do you have that silly grin on your face?"

"Oh, it's nothing," I told her. "You wouldn't believe it anyway."

autumn

"The air felt cool on my cheeks as I walked around my neighbor-hood one sunny fall day, and I noticed that once lush, green trees have transitioned to the bright colors of autumn. I could hear the freshly fallen leaves crunch under my moccasins. The ground was covered by a quilt of orange, brown, burgundy, and yellow, with occasional green grass poking through the leaf cover where the wind had temporarily lifted the colorful blanket up in the air, only to scatter it back on the ground in different places..."

So wrote my seventeen-year-old self, in high school, in Czechoslovakia, during the Cold War era. Both are no more, and I am presently on the other side of the divide, in America.

At the time I thought of myself as a talented writer and I felt hurt when the teacher gave me a B for my flowery effort. At the bottom of the last page the teacher wrote: "When you get closer to the autumn of your life, your passion for the season will diminish."

I thought it was an odd comment, even allowing that I had my nose out of place for getting a B. With the self-righteous wisdom of a seventeen-year-old, I decided that the teacher was wrong. Subconsciously, which later progressed to consciously, I monitored my feelings toward the season.

Whenever possible, in the fall, as I learned to call the season in America, I would drive to see the foliage. Columbus Day weekend was a perfect time for my outings, and when my cousin Elenka invited me to visit her in Whitehall, I was thrilled, because I knew her house was on the border of New York and Vermont.

* * *

Elenka's daughter, Susie, had discovered Whitehall. Ski enthusiasts since their college days, together with her husband, Peter, they fell in love with the area. Its proximity to Killington Mountain was the major draw. They bought a small house and built on it as their family grew.

When it was time to retire, Elenka and her husband, Eddie, bought the house next door.

"We liked our neighbors," my cousin told me, with a wide smile.

My son Danny took the opportunity to get out of NYC and drove with me to Whitehall. As we were about to pull into the driveway, we saw Peter and Susie walking their dog, Chester. My dog, Barney, who had traveled with us, jumped eagerly out of the car and bonded with Chester.

Soon, we were driving toward Killington in Susie's car, a large van they called the Queen Mary. We all piled into the QM, which seated seven or more passengers and, most importantly, could climb the hills around Killington without much effort. As if to show off, QM turned one of the hairpin corners and started the steep ascent up toward the mountain.

The afternoon sun illuminated the beauty that surrounded us. The slopes of the gentle, rolling range of mountains cradled the many streams that ran down their sides. Like an embroidery on a fashion gown, the trees decorated each link of the mountain range in rich colors; from pumpkin orange and the deep, velvet red of peony to all shades of coffee: from the latté to the dark brown with an occasional sprinkle of dark chocolate.

But nothing could surpass the gold of the maple trees, shining brilliantly, as if to memorialize the warmth of a summer's day in the season past.

In order to see the pine trees covering the mountain peaks like a spiky green hat, we needed to take the gondola to the top of the mountain. Alas, we were denied the panoramic view from the top. The gondolas needed repair and were not running that day.

But we would not be defeated and elected to walk up the mountain, as far as possible. With the sun slowly descending, we were treated to a kaleidoscope of constantly changing colors. The angle of the sun's rays would alter the soft green of the pine trees, transforming them into the camouflage on a soldier's khakis. Red leaves changed into the many shades of the pomegranate seed, while gold became cocoa on a winter's day.

The higher we climbed, the more I felt as if I could reach out and stroke the hills around me. I was glad the gondola did not work. We would not have seen the magical effects of the setting sun. For that brief moment, I felt invincible. I breathed deeply, as if to store the crispy clear air in an imaginary vault in my lungs.

During our descent, I put my hands in the pockets of my parka. The departure of the sun made them cold, a sure sign that the snow season was not too far away.

QM took us all safely down to Whitehall. Chester and Barney greeted us with loving enthusiasm. Peter started the fire in the fireplace while Susie put dinner on the table. The dogs were fed and walked and it was time for the Homo Sapiens to eat.

The hum of the conversation around the dining table gave my mind permission to wander. I looked at my cousin Elenka, and I was fascinated how much her wide smile reminded me of my father. She had his signature thick, dark hair with nary a gray, which, sadly, I did not inherit.

We grew up an ocean apart, and we did not meet until we were both adults, yet here I was looking at the familiar features of my father.

The sweet smell of homemade apple pie drew me out of my reverie. Plate and fork in hand, I sat by the fireplace, where Eddie offered me a glass of wine. The dogs searched for the crumbs under the table while the younger generation went to bed. I watched the timber burn and crumble, sending noisy sparks inside the fireplace.

"One for the road?" Eddie asked and I nodded. Elenka stayed with her cup of coffee.

"Just like my father," I thought. He too could drink an espresso and fall asleep as soon as he finished, often before, whereas I would not sleep for a week. We finished our drinks and I closed the door behind my cousins, who drove the short distance to their house next door.

I switched off the lights and put away my empty glass. I knelt beside the two snoring dogs, scratching each behind their ears. Out of the window, lit by the exterior spotlight, my eyes caught the burgundy, gold, and brown leaves as they danced in the gentle wind, on their way to the ground. I thought of my long-ago school effort describing fall and concluded that nothing had changed... only the color of my hair.

the playgroup

When I officially became an adult, I left my home in Czecho-slovakia, sans flowers in my hair, but with starry eyes and impossibly high expectations. I believed that we, the new generation, were for love not war. We were free spirits, and we believed in flower power.

In time, we cut our hair and immersed ourselves in building a future, and with it, as women, we faced the age-old predicament: family or career.

For a long time, I had a perfect excuse for not making a decision. The transient status of my young family gave me an excuse not to dig in too deep. But once it became clear that we were in New Jersey to stay, I began what would become a life-changing transition. Having a new baby and the cancer scare helped me put it all into perspective.

Friends played an important role.

When we bought our house in New Jersey, we needed a lawyer. The real estate agent introduced my husband to Roger. Everyone knows about love at first sight; well, this was an instant and still-lasting friendship. His wife, Jillian, introduced me to her circle of friends. Soon I discovered that out of the small circle of six friends, three would have a new baby within six months. Jillian organized a weekly get-together for the six of us with our children from nine a.m. to eleven a.m. We rotated houses for our meetings. The older children would play while we supported and encouraged each other over some tea or coffee. We discussed the new methods of readying our babies for their entry to the ever-changing world. Or in some cases, going back to the old one, like making our own food instead of buying the Gerber jars. We experimented with the cloth diapers and letting children feed themselves.

As the babies turned to toddlers, our conversations became longer and our time together stretched to twelve-ish. We started to share recipes and interesting magazine articles. We continued to linger longer and soon we included lunch. A future that would include work became a returning topic. Did we want to pick up our abandoned careers or start a new one?

The casual conversations turned serious when the children became old enough to attend kindergarten. We no longer had a reason to meet for lunch. We took turns hosting dinners once a month instead. The men agreed to babysit for us. The husbands and the children referred to us as The Playgroup. We discussed books, politics, and the future. This was a child-free space we dedicated to ourselves.

First to step up to the working world was Nancy. She was a trained ICU nurse with impressive credentials from the University of Virginia. Nancy loved her chosen profession and she knew well the scope and the demands of the job. She was a positive person but also a realistic one. After much analysis, she came to the conclusion that her two boys' involvement in sports would make it difficult to be on a rotating schedule. Always eager to learn, she studied, took her exam, and got a real estate license. Not only was she successful as an agent herself, she started her own very successful real estate agency. Her success was all the more remarkable because she did it alone. Her husband lost his job and never found a new one, making her the breadwinner.

Astri served in local government on the zoning board for fourteen years, four of them as a chair. Later she ran for a seat on the Borough Council and won. She ran on: snowplowing, garbage service, and fixing roads, which are neither Republican nor Democrat issues; they are our issues. In Madison, New Jersey, Astri has the distinction of being the longest-serving councilwoman. She received commendations from her state legislator as well as her congresswoman.

Aggie, our naturalist, started to make flower for charity events and friends' weddings. She started in her kitchen, but as the flowers took over more and more often, she moved to a garage and ended up owning a prominent flower shop on Main Street. To have flowers done by Aggie, you have to book at least six months in advance.

Before children, Kathy had a consulting job with *Newsweek*, where the formidable Katherine Graham, the renowned publisher of *The Washington Post*, took her under her wing. Ms. Graham took Kathy to little-known SoHo galleries in the days when they were merely warehouses in disrcpair, where Ms. Graham introduced Kathy to the works of artists like Jim Dime and Andy Warhol. But Kathy's daughter suffered with asthma and traveling to New York on a daily basis was not possible. But she was a Jersey girl and with her knowledge of the area she soon became a top real estate seller handling some pretty famous future residences of the Garden State.

Jillian, who studied art in college, went back to school and earned a certification necessary to teach art in a local school. Once her children finished their education, she and Roger moved to Maine. She became a full-time artist and opened an art gallery. She is now a well-established local artist and thanks to the internet, she is selling her art all over the US.

I adopted a beautiful dog called Barney. He was the most loving dog I have ever met. I began to wonder who would let go of such a loving companion. I started to picture different scenarios and I started to write them down. The Barney stories were well received by family and friends. With my English much improved, writing brought back the joy I once felt as a teenager. I decided to poke the sleeping bear and I wrote an essay called *Jackie, Nina and I*, which impressed my children, who encouraged me to take some writing courses.

"You were always a storyteller," my son told me.

"Really? You liked my stories?" I was surprised.

I pondered the situation and signed up for an online course. I was lucky to have a great teacher who became a mentor. Armed with my newfound confidence, I enrolled at the NYU School for Continuing Education and took creative non-fiction classes. With much help from spellcheck I had my first essay accepted for publication by bioStories and I finally became a writer.

As our generation became the Baby Boomer generation, our Playgroup reinvented themselves and became successes. I observed, however, that for all the burned brassieres of our youth, we were still very much our mothers' daughters, few of whom had the opportunity to have both, the career and family. Our little group aimed higher than our mothers, but we accepted the limitations when faced with them. But when the time came, we all reinvented ourselves and we succeeded in the most important goal. To give our daughters every opportunity and support to achieve their ambition, whatever it might be.

The Playgroup still meets as often as we can, whether it is in New York, in Maine, New Jersey, or on Cape Cod. We all make the effort to get together. Among the many subjects we talk about, and there are many, is our most important legacy; our guilt-free daughters.

angels among us

Twisting the champagne flute in my fingers, I look around the simple room knowing, of course, that nothing in the Museum of Modern Art is quite what it seems. We are here at MoMA to celebrate the tenth anniversary of the Preston Robert Tish Brain Tumor Center at Duke University.

I search the room for familiar faces to say hello. The atmosphere is one of cerebral elegance that only an institution like MoMA can provide. Hiding behind the minimalist effect are years of hard work and frustration. Just like the artists, the doctors and scientists at Duke have put a lot of hard work behind every tiny step of success. I see my friend Debby and walk over to say hello, just as the lights dim and it all comes back.

Life was moving along nicely for my friend Debby and me until the day when everything disintegrated into one word: Glioblastoma.

I had never heard the word before, nor did I imagine that, one day, I would be helping to wage war on a deadly brain tumor, one that indiscriminately kills men, women, and children.

I became friends with Debby, my neighbor in New Jersey, when our daughters were toddlers. They were born only two months apart, and we were bonded not just by geography, but also by the friendship between our golf-obsessed husbands. Not to mention our dogs.

Debby's dog, Princess, was a beautiful, well-trained Golden Retriever; my beloved Spitz, a spoiled mutt with an attitude. Walking our dogs one cold December morning, we shared the latest insensitivities of our husbands. With the holidays fast approaching, (Hanukah for Debby, Christmas for me), we were busy with the usual chores and projects of mum and CEO of our respective households. I no longer remember the infractions our husbands had committed that day but, whatever they were, it made us feel underappreciated. So, we gave each other the support we felt we deserved, and we created a "Mutual Admiration Society" (M.A.S.), the tongue-in-cheek name belying the closeness of our bond.

Debbie and I were the founding and permanent members of the M.A.S., but we also had many temporary members. We welcomed all women who wished to walk and talk with us— whether they had a dog or not.

One morning Debby mentioned that her husband was having health issues. A trained trauma-unit nurse with a God-given calm and positive personality, she could make it sound like a headache. But when she called for a special M.A.S. meeting, I got a knot in my stomach. I put the leash on Spitz, who was pleased to go on an unscheduled walk.

As soon as the dogs finished their greeting ritual, Debby declared, without frills, "Jon had a brain scan yesterday. He has a brain tumor." My mouth opened and closed without a sound, so she continued, "He is scheduled for surgery next week."

The M.A.S. changed to the M.S.S.: Mutual Support Society. On the day of the surgery, I walked my dog, alone and worried. The time moved at a glacial pace. Finally, the phone rang.

"The good news is that they got the whole tumor out," said Debby into the phone, "the bad news is that it is Glioblastoma."

"Glioblastoma?" I replied, not understanding.

"Glioblastomas always come back," Debby explained.

There was silence while she gave me time to digest this information: her inner nurse was dealing with a shocked relative.

"Oh my God," was all that I could muster.

"We are going to the Duke University Brain Tumor Center as soon as Jon gets out of the hospital. It is the best brain tumor center in the world."

"Tell me what I can do. Anything, anything at all. I can walk Princess, drive Alex to school, whatever you need. I am here for you."

"I know you are," she said.

Two weeks later Spitz and I headed out to meet Debby for our morning walk. She and Jon had come home from Duke the night before, and I was anxious to hear the news. As Debby and Princess walked toward me, I sensed a newfound hope in my friend's step.

"They started treatment right away." She seemed pleased. "This treatment may afford him three to five years. Even more if we are lucky."

She looked at me as if I should bc pleased. Registering my look of shock, she added, "Otherwise he would have three, maybe five months."

We walked in silence. After a while, I asked if there was anything I could do, but I feared I had little to offer.

"You organize fundraisers, right?" She seemed to be thinking aloud. "So, do one for Duke."

"I will..."

"The time is now," she said.

It was the first time in our friendship that I had seen Debbie impatient.

The co-president of our newly rechristened M.S.S. looked me in the eye. "It may not help Jon, but it could save others."

She was the nurse again and she had realistic expectations.

"Or we will fight and win," I countered, ever the optimist.

"That, too, is a possibility," the nurse conceded, allowing herself a bit of hope and a smile.

And with that, in the gentle hills of New Jersey, the war against Glioblastoma was on.

We planned the first golf tournament at a place Jon loved with a passion: the Baltusrol Golf Club. The club had witnessed all of his triumphs—in Jon's mind, there were no disappointments. For Jon, playing golf was always filled with triumphs, each one varying in degree, but triumphs nonetheless. A doctor and a scientist in the field of infectious diseases, Jon was a man who did serious work, yet he retained an almost childlike passion for all that life had to offer. He dressed perfectly, carrying himself well in his somber, elegant fashion.

His love for his family could not be surpassed even by his love of golf. To Jon, everything his children did was remarkable. It could have seemed silly if it was not so genuine. As a doctor, he had seen a lot of pain and sadness, so, to him, life was a gift to be savored and treasured.

Once we started to work on the tournament, the support poured in. Jon was known as a generous man. At times, he was even taken advantage of—though he never saw it that way. To Jon, kindness was unconditional and, therefore, impossible to abuse. The overwhelming support that his name now triggered was a testimony to that conviction.

In the difficult months following Jon's diagnosis, he made several trips to Duke for his treatment. By the time we held our first tournament, his hair (most of which he lost during the treatment), had started to grow back. Jon looked more like himself again. But he was on "Duke time," borrowed by virtue of his treatment.

Dr. Henry Friedman, who treated Jon, came to meet with the donors at the tournament. During dinner, he spoke to an audience of men and women, most of whom knew very little about brain tumors. They came to play golf and support a friend, but they left educated about how deadly an adversary glioblastoma is and how elusive its cure continues to be. He spoke about the experimental treatment that Jon was undergoing while Jon beamed, looking in miraculous good health.

The fundraiser was a huge success. I viewed the tournament as a one-off fundraiser. My expertise was in organizing more conventional fundraisers—dinner, an auction (preferably with some interesting slant), or a fashion show with some entertainment. *There* I knew what I was doing. So, when donors started to say how they were looking forward to the next year, I worried. Golf was not my game; I mean, I provoked hilarity by asking where the blinkers were on the golf carts.

A few months after our golf fundraiser, another neighbor, Don Parcells, was diagnosed with a brain tumor. At the time I did not know him, but I knew that our children went to the same schools. I realized I had better embrace golf pronto, and I booked the outing for the next year.

For the second tournament, I added some touches of my own. We organized small, informal modeling sessions during the cocktail hour, for those attending only the dinner and auction portion of the fundraiser.

Dr. Ian Smith, a medical correspondent with NBC and a friend from fashion-show fundraisers I had organized in the past, emceed the festivities. When he asked if he could bring a friend, I told him it would be my pleasure. And indeed it was. The friend turned out to be Mike Strahan, the defensive end for the New York Giants. Mike joked with Don Parcells about the hard time his brother Bill was giving him during football practice.

As I watched their friendly banter, I was struck by the intensity of Don's eyes. They were silver-blue in the morning, but, as the sun fell low on the horizon, his eyes mirrored the sun's fire. He was ready to fight for his life.

During the whole evening, Mike was gracious beyond words; listening to Monday-morning quarterbacks with patience and humor and signing autographs long after the event was over.

But the cruel foe had made itself present and after the fourth year, we lost Don Parcells. During that time, another great man lost his battle with glioblastoma and the Duke Research Center was renamed in his memory: Preston Robert Tisch Brain Tumor Research Center.

Jon never stopped believing in his treatment, although he did have to stop working. Typically, he turned this setback into a positive and used his time to take golf lessons. By the fifth year of the tournament, we had raised enough money for a professorship, which meant that Duke could hire another scientist for the research.

A few weeks after the fifth tournament, Jon made an unscheduled trip to Duke. The glioblastoma was back.

Again, Jon fought hard for his life. He was between treatments and home in Short Hills when my husband and I drove from New York City, where we had recently moved, to see him and Debby. Jon seemed fine to me, but I noticed that Debby was watching his every move. We talked about golf and our daughters, who had recently graduated from high school yet remained best friends.

When we stood to leave, Jon walked us to the door. He hugged me as he said goodbye. I noticed that he swayed a bit. I told myself that perhaps it was caused by his medication. Then he extended his hand to my husband for a handshake.

Turning to the man he had spent the last fifteen years playing golf and sharing family milestones with, he said, "Thank you for coming. Now remind me, who are you?"

My husband did not miss a beat and told him his name, but I could not look at Debby for fear of crying. We drove silently all the way to New York City.

A few weeks later, Debby called to ask if I wanted to have lunch in the old neighborhood. I was excited because she sounded as if she had something to say. I hoped for good news, forgetting how calm she could be in crises. We met for lunch and, as usual, she got right to the point.

"Would you like to come and see Jon?" she asked.

I rolled my eyes to communicate that it was an unnecessary question.

"He does not come downstairs often, but today he is down. So, I thought you would like to see him. He is not the same, you know," she warned.

When we walked into the familiar living room, the television was on but Jon appeared to be sleeping. His children were around him and said hello. I told myself he had always been slim. But when he opened his eyes, I was not sure he knew who I was.

I started to talk just to break the silence. He smiled and gestured for me to sit next to him. I talked about the golf tournament for the next year, and I could see that he had understood me, made the connection. I was sure he knew who I was. Then he fell asleep again. When I was leaving, I said goodbye to him, but he seemed to be asleep. Then, just as I opened the door, he opened his eyes, stretched his hand toward me, and waved.

Three weeks later came the inevitable call that Jon had lost his battle. He was buried on a sunny summer day. I could almost hear him remark, "A great day for golf."

Our last golf tournament honored Jon and Don and all the people, unknown to us but loved by their family and friends, who fought bravely but lost the unevenly matched battle with a merciless foe.

Debby and I remained committed to Duke. Debby took her husband's place on the board of advisors. I was honored with an invitation to one of the board's meetings. We visited the hospital and the Preston Robert Tisch Research Center. It was at the hospital where I learned that brain tumors occur in people of all ages but, statistically, they are more common in children and older adults.

When we toured the laboratory, I was able to see the formidable glioblastoma under the microscope. I had an overwhelming urge to flush it down the toilet, to avenge all the people that had so much to live for. If only it were that simple.

Patients from thirty-five states are treated at Duke annually.

Although many do lose their fight, there are also survivors. I was lucky to meet one of them: Sandy Hillburn.

In 2010, we held a fundraiser in New York City and Sandy agreed to come and talk about her five-year battle with glioblastoma. In describing her fight, the feisty, petite women from Fort Lee, New Jersey, clenched her fist and told us how she finds the prognosis unacceptable and how—with Dr. Friedman's treatment and Duke's dedication to conquer the tumor—she intends to win.

Like Jon, Sandy also had the humor and tenderness that made everyone root for her. She was the perfect antidote after all the people we had lost.

* * *

AT THE SPICEHANDLER INVITATIONAL — From left are organizers and supporters of the April 14 fourth annual Spicehandler Invitational, from left Dr. Ian Smith, Sterrin Bird, Don Parcells, Jarmila Sullivan, Mike Strahan and Dr. Jon Spicehandler.

Dr. Friedman's voice brings me back to MoMA. "Let me introduce Sandy Hillburn, who was diagnosed ten years ago..."

I have not seen Sandy in five years, but she has lost none of her spark. On the contrary, she is feisty, even challenging. As she finishes her speech, I blow her kisses and she waves back.

I look around and I know that everyone in that room and thousands who are not, were all part of her success story, because each survivor is a step toward victory. It is appropriate that it is in a simple room at MoMA, a place where, as we all know, nothing is as it seems and surprise is to be expected.

still lucky

At about the time I was a toddler crawling on the floor of our kitchen/living room in Communist Czechoslovakia, a young man was crawling across enemy ground halfway around the world. The biggest dangers for me were my two older brothers, who might not see me and step on my fingers. For him, the slightest mistake would cost him his life.

Eddie was born in the First Czechoslovak Republic, but his parents made it out to America just before Hitler put his big boot on the little country in the heart of Europe. So when Eddie turned eighteen years old, he was proud to go and defend his new country in Korea.

When I graduated from crawling to walking, I learned that my father had a sister in America. Not an unusual phenomenon in Czechoslovakia, where most families had some relatives who went to America to look for work.

In the black-and-white world of Communism, a color photograph of my cousin Elenka holding her baby, Susie, etched itself in my eleven-year-old mind. She stood in a snow-covered garden. Her dark hair and her red lips contrasted with the white snow. Her smile made my spirit soar. She had married that young man of Slovak heritage called Eddie when he came back from Korea.

After a spin of the globe, and time, I met my cousin Elenka and her husband, Eddie, in America, just across the George Washington Bridge from New York City. Eddie and Elenka were delighted that I had married an American, albeit a Red Sox fan.

Thus it was that family members once divided by geography and politics became closer, and our ties grew stronger. Eddie never spoke about Korea. He talked about the Yankees and Red Sox instead.

After Eddie and Elenka retired, they moved to Whitehall on the border of Vermont and New York. I was thrilled when I received an invitation to visit them one Columbus Day weekend, so that I could see the leaves turn into a kaleidoscope of colors. My son's desire to come with me, I suspected, was more due to the memory of barbeques at Eddie and Elenka's house in New Jersey and their specialty, the Slovak klobasy.

Baby Susie, in the color photograph, grew up, got married, and had three boys, one of whom was my son's age. She was thrilled to give us a tour of the area in that large station wagon she and her husband named the Queen Mary. By the time we got back to Eddie and Elenka's house, we could smell the klobasy before we opened the door.

After a mouthwatering dinner, three different generations were sitting close to the fireplace when I noticed a picture of Eddie in his US Army uniform. I had never seen it before and could not take my eyes off it.

Korea: the forgotten war.

My son followed my eyes to the photograph and asked Eddie, "What was the Korean War like?"

"Like? There was nothing to 'like' about it. It was serious business. Horrible."

He paused and realized that all eyes were on him. Reluctantly, he continued.

"I was a member of the 19th Infantry Regiment with the 24th Division. I was the FO. Forward Observer. It was my job to spot the North Koreans and let our guys know where to shoot. Behind me were six big guns. The distance between the guns and

Eddie during Korean War

me changed periodically, depending on how far I had to go to spot the North Koreans.

"I also had to watch our planes. They were above me, also looking for the enemy. From above, they could not tell who was down there. I had to put out colored blankets around me so that our pilots knew not to shoot me. The North Koreans tried to see what color we were putting out and used the same color so that their FO could get close to us. So, we changed the color of our blankets frequently.

"Mistakes were deadly. Sometimes you did not have to make a mistake—just bad luck—and still wound up dead. The terrain was harsh and we were not familiar with it. I had two men with me: a radioman, who would pass on the information I gathered to the guns behind us, and one man with an automatic rifle to protect me. But when I was spotting, I was alone. A single man had a better chance not to be seen. We would be in the terrain for two weeks and then have two weeks at the command quarters."

Eddie's voice trailed off. I noticed his short, halting sentences, as if the caution he had exercised in Korea had entered his consciousness again.

"Fellow soldiers became close friends," he continued after that pause. "We depended on one another. My FO alternate and I understood each other. We knew what was out there. The silence was worse than the gunfire. He was from California and had a two-month-old baby.

"One day, he did not come back. I was sent to find him. I came across a body strung to a tree, used for shooting practice. Very cautiously, I removed the dead soldier's dog tags; I had found my friend. I wrapped the dog tags with a string to ensure they would not make a sound against each other. No sense to give the enemy another target for practice. I tried not to think about my friend, but I could not escape the fact that far away in California a child would grow up without a father."

As Eddie paused, the only sound came from the wood burning in the fireplace.

"The death and danger were everywhere. You had to suppress the human impulse to help another human being. When we came across a wounded enemy soldier, the procedure was not to touch him. Most of them had explosives attached to their bodies, and they would activate them as soon as we got close. Today's suicide bombers did not invent that tactic."

I pictured Eddie, the peaceful, churchgoing young man, who in his native New Jersey would not kill a fly, leaving another human being to die because he knew that person would kill him for his kindness. It had to be a hard lesson to learn.

"One time, we captured a Korean FO who turned out to be a woman, " Eddie continued with a somewhat lighter tone. "The usual procedure was to strip the soldier naked after tying his hands to prevent him from detonating explosives, if he had any, and then neutralize the explosives. We started to strip the woman but, for a moment, we hesitated. We were all young men, boys, really, mostly around twenty, and stripping a woman, even an enemy woman, elicited a few nervous giggles."

He laughed a bit nervously. Even after all those years.

Eddie caught us looking at him as if there were more to the story.

"I know, not quite what a movie today would do with the story," he quipped. It was our turn to laugh nervously.

"Perhaps it was because we knew so many South Korean women who helped us. I tell you, some of the tiniest women carried as much heavy equipment as any of us did. We respected them and we were grateful for their help."

Elenka held Eddie's hand, making sure that this time, she shared the difficult journey with her husband. Suddenly I realized there are only a few of those young men still alive, and I was privileged to hear one of the seldom-told stories.

"I was lucky," Eddie concluded. Then, bringing Elenka's hand to his lips, he added, "I am lucky."

Indeed still lucky

Still Lucky, was published by *Ariel Chart International Literary Journal,* in its November 3, 2021 issue.

an unfulfilled dream

Through the COVID-19 lockdown in spring 2020, people were buying everything in sight. During a visit to my local supermarket, the empty shelves brought on a memory. In my youth, in Communist Czechoslovakia, empty shelves were the norm, not the result of a pandemic.

That memory flooded in. I had to put my hand over my still-unmasked mouth to hide the smile as I joined a line of people waiting for a new supply of toilet paper. I came back to the apartment empty-handed and told my husband how we dealt with toilet paper shortages back then.

Under Communism, toilet paper was quite often a scarce item. There was never enough of it to store up, so we used newspapers. We children were tasked with tearing the pages of the newspaper into squares, then crushing them in our hands before putting them into a shoebox that was then taken to the WC and placed within easy reach for the occupant of the throne. The idea was to make the paper softer and to get most of the ink on our hands, which we washed much more often than our behinds.

There were certain pieces, with photographs of the government officials and members of the Communist Party, that my father kept for himself. And the pages with Brezhnev and his Czechoslovak lackeys' pictures on them, he saved for special occasions. My father was lactose intolerant but loved cheese. Every so often he would bow to the demands of his tastebuds, with the predictable results. Then it was Brezhnev and his crew's time.

My American husband was astonished by my story and rejected the idea on the grounds that the newspaper would block the drains, though I have to say he scored points in my book because he did not object to the idea, in principle, of using the newspaper. Perhaps there were particular politicians he had in mind. There was no doubt in my mind who my present-day Brezhnev and his enablers would be. Thanks to the narrow pipes of our civilized nation, however, such justice has remained but a dream.

Unfulfilled Dream was published on Jun 29, 2021 by *Cleaver*, Philadelphia's International Literary Magazine.

see you

The early hours at an airport are usually dreary, but never more than after an overnight flight in the middle of January. I sat at the Vienna airport and sipped the famous Viennese coffee to warm me up while I waited for my three adult children, who were arriving from different parts of the US.

There was not much time to plan the journey to my brother Pavel's funeral. I wondered what it was that made my children come to tiny Slovakia in the middle of winter. One of them could only get away for forty-eight hours, yet they were compelled to come and say goodbye to an uncle they met only a few times in their lives.

The small living room was full of relatives I had not seen in many years. Everyone spoke in hushed voices out of respect for the occasion, but I knew they were also curious to see their American relatives.

"The last time I have seen you, you were a little boy," said my cousin to my son, whose six-foot-four-inch frame towered over her. He understood enough Slovak to know what she was saying, and smiled.

"How the time flies," she said to me with tears in her eyes. I nodded. The news of my brother's passing was not a surprise. He was not well for some time, we knew, although he'd downplayed his illness.

In Slovakia, where Pavel still lived, we were trained to underplay our pain for the sake of the people around us, but those left behind were allowed to let their sorrow show fully once the brave person passed away. Although I have spent most of my adult life in America, I have a very hard time controlling my emotions at any given funeral. I would cry uncontrollably at the funeral for relatives of my husband whom I barely knew. I suspect I was taking the opportunity to mourn all those whose funerals I have missed because of politics or the distance.

My brother Pavel had just turned seventy and was too young to die. He was the middle child of three, with me being the youngest. My mother used to say that Pavel's eyes were made of quicksilver. Always dancing with a twinkle and mischief. I remembered when he played street hockey with neighborhood boys using an old sardine can as a puck. The boys were told repeatedly not to use the cans lying around on the streets. After the rusty can gashed Pavel's eyebrow, just above his right eye, he would not give his friends away when he was asked for their names. He felt pretty sure that seven stitches in his forehead guaranteed him immunity from any punishment.

Children in Communist Czechoslovakia were divided into two groups: athletes and artists. Pavel was a great athlete. He was not just a swimmer or hockey player or runner, he did it all. Still in his twenties, he ran in an internationally attended Kosice marathon that my mother watched on TV. Exhausted and stumbling, Pavel pushed himself close to the camera and waved, because he knew his mother was watching.

It was Pavel who was with me in Prague when I was leaving for England for the first time. He pressed a pocket-size English/Slovak dictionary into my hand saying, "You'll need it." Just before I disappeared behind the airport's gate of no return, I turned around, looked at him, and heard him say, "See you."

Later, when I was an established model in London, making my way into television, Pavel visited me and I took him to the studio to see the taping of a show I was in. The French singer Charles Aznavour, whom I knew, was there to sing his hit song "She." I introduced my brother to him. Later, I saw them in deep conversation. They spoke in French, in which Pavel was fluent, but when I reached them, Pavel switched to English because he knew I did not speak French.

Before I moved to America, I was in New York to shoot a TV commercial and I fell in love with the city. I sent Pavel a postcard. Czechoslovakia was still in the iron grip of the Soviet Union, but I wrote to him, "I don't know when and I don't know how, but I promise you I will make sure that you will visit this magical city." When he did come to New York many years later, he brought the postcard with him, ever my treasure.

Family drove to the cemetery in a taxi while everyone else walked. I was glad for the few relatively alone moments so that I could say goodbye to my brother. The most vivacious person I had ever known did not move, did not smile. His eyes were closed, and I knew, had no twinkle in them.

I sat in the pew, resting my forehead on my hands. I would try not to embarrass my American children by allowing the sorrow to overtake me. So, I focused on the long-gone days when the three of us climbed the big cherry tree in our yard in the summer, burned leaves in the fall, and skated on frozen streets in the winter. But the face without a smile, neat mustache, a signature oversized bowtie and the jacket from the suit his father made for him for his wedding was superimposing itself over the childhood memories.

I felt a tap on one of the hands upon which I rested my head. "Do you remember me?" asked a woman my age who I remembered going to high school with. We were good friends, but we did not stay in touch. In those days it was not prudent to have correspondence with someone in the "West." I did not blame her.

"Yes, Lena," I said.

"We'll talk later," she said and sat somewhere behind me in the packed church. In our high school days, nobody would have dared to go to church for a wedding, christening, or funeral. Things have changed, but I still appreciated that she came.

I put my head back on my hands and the night Pavel and I drank the last stash of Dad's Slivovice, the night etched deep in my heart, came into focus. I was back in Communist Czechoslovakia for the first time since Jan, the eldest of the three of us, emigrated to England.

Before Jan left, he knew that his defection would have potentially negative consequences for Pavel. To minimize the impact, Jan decided not to tell Pavel about his plans. He knew Pavel was a bad liar and assumed he would be asked what he knew about his brother's defection. Not knowing would let him honestly reply in the negative.

When Jan took the job with the BBC World Service, it was bittersweet. Mother was proud of her oldest son being a broadcaster for the BBC, but for Pavel it meant further repercussions, which he had to keep from his ailing mother. Perhaps it was a cruel blessing that not long after, she entered her last battle with cancer, sparing her the Sophie's choice and Pavel the pretending.

"It's the last one," Pavel said that night as he put the bottle on the table. He poured us each a generous glass. I eyed it, then went to the kitchen and brought us each a glass of water. "To hydrate," I said.

"You mean to dilute. Some stuff cannot be diluted." He drank the first shot. "I listen to him every night," he added. I knew who he was talking about. "He should have told me that he was not coming back."

"He tried to protect you," I said.

Pavel looked at me with glistening eyes, and I knew it was not a product of the Slivovica.

"Well, I lost my job at the reception anyway."

I said nothing.

"Because I would not spy for them." Pavel looked at me as tears ran down his handsome cheeks.

The spa where my brother worked had a lot of foreign guests. Most were from Austria, Germany, France, England, and the USA. Pavel was fluent in all three languages.

"I was to keep notes about who the foreigners met with, where they went, and engage them on topics I'd be supplied with, and report back...I wouldn't do it."

He told me all the threats and innuendo he had to deal with. I knew most of it already, but he needed to tell me, so I listened.

The next day, when the airplane lifted me up toward the sky and back to my home in England, I thought about the night before and my brother Pavel. He did not blame me or Jan. He was not angry for being left behind. Twice. First, after the terrible day in August 1968 as the Soviet tanks were raping the country, when my father told him to stay in Czechoslovakia because he did not want to burden me, and then when our brother, Jan, left. Maybe it was his acceptance that made the Soviet tanks roll over my heart again.

"Mum, get up." My son was lifting me gently out of the pew. I looked up and saw that the church was empty. I walked to face the people, some of whom would be strangers to me. When I stepped out of the church, I saw hundreds of them waiting to shake my hand and tell me their micro stories: how Pavel drove a friend with a broken leg to the hospital, shoveled an elderly neighbor's driveway in a snowstorm, gave a pack of Dunhill cigarettes to a man who hoped only for the filter-less local ones, a couple for whom he played Cupid, now married thirty-five years, a truly selfless hockey player, a widow whose child he always found time to talk to...

I watched the mourners walk toward the town, and above their heads I saw Pavel's smiling face disappearing into the distance. For just a split moment, our eyes met.

"See you," I said.

Last time together

the thanksgiving table

Melting away the darkness, the sun came up as I drove from New York City to Cape Cod. My friend Katrina sat next to me sipping coffee. This was not our first trip together, going back to our journey when she drove me to the hospital after I was diagnosed with cancer, now thankfully far in the rearview mirror.

We first met in Frankfurt where Katrina, after a successful career as a model, became one of the founders of a film company specializing in making TV commercials. She cast me to be the model for Close Up, the first not white, pink, nor baby-blue toothpaste. It was in fact bright red in color.

Thanksgiving was on the horizon, and I was determined to get the rosewood dining room table I had in our summer home to my son, who had just moved with his young family from a small apartment in New York City to his first house in Connecticut. Both the table and my son originated in Hong Kong, when my husband and I briefly lived there, so naturally I felt he should have the table once I did not have a need for it.

Despite the flu shot I'd received a couple of weeks earlier, it had become painful to swallow by the time we reached Massachusetts. Mind over matter, I told myself. We arrived at Harwich Port, and I got right to work. I hosed down the dirt of the past summer off the back of the truck, then with Katrina's help we disassembled the oval-shaped table for eight into a round table for four. I wrapped the two leaves in an old bedsheet for protection and lined up the chairs against the wall, ready to be transported. I went to bed satisfied and ready for an early morning departure.

I was awakened by Katrina singing, "Hey ho, hey ho, it's off to the work we go," while handing me a cup of coffee. At our age, getting up early is often more the decision of one's bladder than of the owner of the organ. Her bladder had five years on mine, so she was up before me. It was still dark outside, and we were on schedule with our plan to leave with the first rays of sun. My throat felt worse, but when I touched my forehead, it did not feel hot. I got dressed before the cold air had the chance to put goosebumps on my skin.

Having assessed which was the shortest way out of the house the night before, Katrina and I set out to get the heavy table through the swinging door that was the entry and exit to the dining room. To an unbiased eye, the space would look too small, but to me it was a matter of geometry. We tried sideways, we tried upside down, we pulled and we pushed. To the Buddha statue perched on the top shelf of the display cabinet, our struggle had to resemble two fools following a dubious logic: it got in there, so it has to be possible to get it out.

Actually measuring the opening against the height of the leg of the table seemed equivalent to admitting defeat, so I ignored the tape measure lying seductively next to the laughing Buddha. We continued the fight: the table versus the door. When my finger got caught between the door and the table, the pain shot to my brain, and I spoke the fatal words.

"The door has to come off." My swollen throat made my voice sound as if it were coming from the depth of Siberia. I banished the thought of the four-hour drive to my son's house and four-hour drive back for later.

I studied my opponent. I had taken down standard doors before, but the swing door, I was learning, had no logic or any obvious clue. Despite removing the top screw, the door would not move sideways, or any other ways. I tried to lift it and realized how heavy it was. Like the wolf straining to blow down the smart pig's house, I huffed and I puffed but got no farther along than the wolf.

Katrina watched in silence, giving no advice or opinion on my method of removing the door, for which I was grateful. But she did hover close, ready to catch the door in case it suddenly surrendered and tried to kill me on its way out.

"The door is leaking," she said in a voice that could have been asking me if I wanted a cup of coffee. I looked down at my feet and indeed there was a small but visible puddle of dark green oil coming somewhere from the secret belly of the door. Katrina, who owns only three types of attire: glamorous, PJ, and bikini, was wiping the puddle at my feet dressed in her usual glam frock. I watched her, wearing old jeans and my husband's discarded sweater.

I could hear the Buddha meditating loudly in my head. "Get the movers to do it." His voice sounded remarkably like my husband's. I rolled my eyes, knowing there was nobody available before Thanksgiving. Besides, who had moved the kids to and from college all those years? I need no advice from you, Mr. Buddha.

If the table was heavy, the door was a deadweight. I tilted it with all the strength I could find in my weakening body and proceeded to whack myself in the head. Before the bump on my noggin had the chance to grow to its full size, I yelled, "Get the hammer."

Solemnly, Katrina handed me the hammer and I smacked the door three times, much harder than I intended to, influenced by the pain inside my head that had been matched by the pain in the bump on my forehead. Suddenly the dark oil squirted on the ceiling, the walls, and onto my face. Like the scene in the movie *Giant* when James Dean struck oil, I saw dollar signs, but mine were going the wrong direction, out of my pocket.

Katrina ran to the kitchen and was back in a flash with an extra-large roll of paper towels. With a surge of strength I did not know I had, fueled purely by desperation, I pulled the door sideways and heard a mighty crack, and finally it let go and its weight told me it was no longer attached to the hinges. I held it close to me like a drunk dancing partner, afraid it would fall, and waltzed with it to the closest wall.

We scrubbed the oil off the ceiling, the walls, and the floor. I ignored the Buddha, who was laughing at me. "Sarcasm is the lowest form of humor," I shot back at him.

We finished cleaning, leaving a few stubborn tell-tales behind on the ceiling, then took a pause to assess the damage and the subsequent rescue effort.

Katrina studied me with a narrowed eye. "There is a man trapped in your head," she said tersely.

"First, we have to get the table onto the truck." I ignored the implicit sexism in her remark. We usually come to the same conclusions, but we get there in different ways.

I went out to move the back of the truck as close to the front door as I could, but there still remained a fair distance. Knowing how heavy the table was, I fetched a wheelbarrow from the shed and wheeled it next to the door. Not very sexy, but functional. With the table wrapped in the fleece blanket, we shimmied it onto the wheelbarrow and moved gingerly toward the truck. Our slow procession looked as if we'd shot a fat deer with skinny legs.

At last, we reached our destination. We pulled and pushed the table, padded by an ample amount of fleece blankets, and managed to get the beast on to the back of the truck, legs up in surrender.

We secured the chairs, which by then felt like skinny relatives.

Despite leaving an hour later than planned, the traffic for which I had calculated did not materialize and we caught up with our timing. We dropped off the table, no door giving us a challenge, and with my son's help, we were soon on our way back.

By the time we crossed the Sagamore Bridge on to Cape Cod, the full moon took over, lighting our way the last half hour on the road. In the eight-hour journey, we never ran out of subjects to discuss. As we neared our destination, food became the subject.

"Oysters and champagne for two macho women," said Katrina.

I looked at her stylish hat and her perfect makeup the squirting oil from the door had not dared to interfere with and agreed. "Yes. Absolutely."

Cape Cod being home to the famous Wellfleet oysters, there was no shortage of places that sold the delicacy. I pulled into the bar closest to my house that happened to have valet parking. When I gave the young man my keys, he looked at the dusty truck and my workman's attire, then at Katrina's glam outfit, and gave me a look that could be interpreted as horror or "cool." I decided on "cool."

After a dozen oysters each later, plus a glass of champagne for Katrina and beer for me, I drove the short distance home, exhausted but happy.

My throat still hurt but was not getting worse. I walked into the empty dining room and the vision of a beautifully set Thanksgiving table now in the Connecticut burbs filled me with pure joy. I looked at the door still standing where I left it in the puddle of oil. Carefully, I removed the rugs, making sure the door was at last dry.

"Don't worry, I will not leave it to all the king's men to put you back together again." I touched the door gently. Lifting my eyes toward the Buddha, I winked at him, saying, "I'll let you pay for it."

In the kitchen, Katrina made me a hot chamomile tea with honey, lots of lemon, and even more whiskey.

"Here is your hot toddy. It will help your throat." Always true to herself, Katrina had put on fresh lipstick and, holding an elegant glass of wine in one hand, she handed me my favorite red mug full of hot liquid. We ate the food my son's wife had wrapped up to take with us.

I raised my glass to my friend.

"May we always have something to be thankful for."

Feeling good, we sat with our feet up on the sofa. Between us, Katrina and I have racked up 149 years in age, and we came to the conclusion that if you got it, don't waste it. And we still had it.

the pram

Sunday summer afternoon on Cape Cod, as a rule, is dedicated to relaxation time. So why am I sweating, cleaning an old pram? Because this is not some secondhand thing my husband dragged in from one of his garage sale expeditions. This is the pram we bought for our first child many years ago in the Mothercare shop on Oxford Street in London. The result of my extended polish brings the pram back to its original splendor. The British Steel stamp shines in the afternoon sun. The navy pram with its white-and-blue-check lining looks pristine.

I squint my eyes and remember the day my husband and I brought the pram to our terraced house in Kew Gardens in our white Ford Cortina.

Memories, once unleashed, flow into the ravine created by time. I think about Mrs. Landis, the woman who made me grow up by throwing me in the deep end, but stood guard, making sure I would not drown.

I think about Finley, whose love for me at the time I could not grasp. But the friendship that came out of that love grounded me and helped me see the future. In return, when Finley began to float toward a drug-infused haze, I suggested he go to Israel to work on a kibbutz. It was an in-vogue thing to do at the time. He trusted my advice and stayed two years. When he came back, he introduced me to an American girl he met at the kibbutz. They stayed at my flat for a week and then went to America. The last correspondence I had with Finley, or rather with his friend Ella, who was from Connecticut, was a letter where she asked me to send her the copy of the divorce certificate, which I did. Not long after, I met my own American, got married, and sold my flat. In the move the letter got lost and so did my contact with Finley. But my gratitude has never left my heart, which is why every year on my birthday I drink a toast to his health and wish him all the best, wherever he might be.

* * *

"Is that my pram?" The voice of the first occupant of the pram, my son Jimmy, brings me back to Cape Cod.

"Yes, it is," I answer, mentally shrinking the six-foot-four young man into a size that would fit into the pram.

"You are not planning to sell it?" my conservationist asks.

"Don't worry, I will keep it for you." I sneak a look at his wife sitting in the shade with a book to see if I can detect the sign of a "baby glow."

I turn back to the pram. The sun's ray touches the newly polished pram's handle and sends a spark toward the sky, blinding me just long enough to remind me of a cloudless September sky when all hearts in the world had skipped a beat and when too many hearts stopped beating forever. September 11, 2001. For days after, from my home in New Jersey, I watched the dark cloud loom over Lower Manhattan.

That day played a pivotal role in my decision to become an immigrant, American immigrant. In the years past, wandering around the world, I always thought of myself as an emigrant with permission to reside in England. After the terrorist attack, I let go of my tie to England, although never the gratitude. I became an American and stood with my new country.

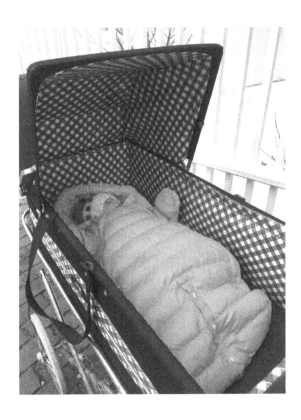

The sun sets behind our neighbor's tall trees and I put the pram inside the house. I see vividly each child as they lay in the pram, all the joy and tribulations ahead. Picturing my three children, I wonder when did they go from "growing up" to "getting older?" When did they stop bickering and start to have conversations without me being a referee? How dare they become so civilized?

The following summer, the pram did have a new occupant. The first of the second generation, my grandson Arthur.

* * *

Winter in Cape Cod has a magic that I believe is available only to those who have the privilege to spend summers there. We see the sleepy brown landscapes and the gray ocean with its winter whitecaps, superimposed on the background of memory from the summers past.

Blue and white hydrangeas, mingling with the knockout roses, decorate the Cape Cod landscape as far as the eye can see. Scrap pines overlook the winding roads as if to protect us from getting lost. The sound of children playing on the beach now mingles with the wind singing in the empty land around the salty inlets throughout Pleasant Bay.

After the success of our first family Christmas gathering, on the Cape, we have decided to make Christmas in Cape Cod a family tradition. On Christmas Eve I make sure that it is as close as possible to the Christmas Eve I described in my letter to my parents, sitting alone in the flat in London, all those years ago. Throwing walnuts into corners aided only by candlelight has been a highlight my children would look forward to through the whole year. Christmas Day is American and my husband is in charge of the turkey. Everybody takes one or two extra days off from work so that we can include the proper British Boxing Day.

I look forward to the arrival of the whole family; the Atheists, the devout Catholics, the Agnostics, and the Innocent.

While the rest of the family go out and look for that last elusive gift, I volunteer to babysit my grandson.

*The itsy bitsy spider climbed up the waterspout. Down came the rain and washed the spider out...*My grandson sings one of his favorite songs. Outside, the hydrangea flowers had turned brown, and I watch their heads bow under the cover of snow.

"Read this, Babka." Arthur pushes his Mr. Happy book into my hand.

"Mr. Happy?" I remember buying Mr. Men books for his father in London and I am pleased that Mr. Men books still reign supreme.

"Yes," comes the resolute answer.

"All right, but first give Babka a big hug." I drive a hard bargain. Arthur snuggles in my arms as I hold the little boy close to my heart and begin, "Mr. Happy..."

jackie, nina, and me

"Travel is the university of life," my mother said with regularity. I thought about her words as I looked out the window into the night, one that started no differently than any other. The moon cast a pale light on the unattractive buildings built quickly by the Communist government in the years following World War II. Speed, not beauty, was of essence as the nation rose from the ashes.

As a teenager, every Friday at eight p.m., I listened to the one radio program that broadcast music and poetry the young people in Communist Czechoslovakia wanted to hear. I listened to *Ave Maria* sung by Charles Aznavour, followed by a poem beautifully written by a fellow teenager. It spoke of love and of hope found in a sliver of a blue sky by two young people trapped in darkness— and in that moment it fostered in me a palpable need to write.

My mind was still processing the words of that poem when the radio program was interrupted by a somber announcement:

*Jackie Kennedy, Nikita Khrushchev, Austrian President Adolf
Schaerf, Nina Khrushchev, John F. Kennedy*

"The American president, John F. Kennedy, has been assassinated in Dallas, Texas." It was eight forty-five p.m.

A single bare light bulb hung from the ceiling of our small family room. It cast a somber glow over the white, freshly ironed tablecloth covering the table where I sat. Above the wooden radio hung a black-and-white photograph of President Kennedy; his wife, Jackie; Soviet Premier Khrushchev; and his wife, Nina Petrovna. I had cut it out from *ZENA* ("WOMAN") magazine and pinned it there after reading an article about the two women—though it was mostly about Nina Petrovna. Jackie was described as "a beautiful woman" and it was implied that, as such, she had no substance. The photograph was taken at a summit held in Vienna more than two years earlier. I stared at the picture in shocked disbelief.

Decades later, that image has remained in my mind. The visual contrast between the two women is marked. Jackie is tall, slim, young, and elegant. She exudes beauty and femininity. In contrast, Nina Petrovna looks matronly, an older woman who has seen hardship, death, and injustice. It was easy to ascribe one word to each woman: to Jackie, beautiful; to Nina Petrovna, babushka.

Looking at the photograph on that November night, I wondered how the two women felt right then, at that tragic moment immediately after the assassination. I imagined Jackie grieving and frightened. But what about Nina Petrovna? Did she close her eyes at least briefly and let the world go dark for a moment so that her heart could go to Jackie?

I knew from the *ZENA* article that Nina Petrovna was born in Ukraine, attended a private boarding school for girls, and received a first-class education. The school normally did not accept the children of peasants, but Nina was able to study at Maryanski Girl's School—writing in her notebook, "I chanced to be there because of the special circumstances of war." She studied political economy in Moscow and later taught it at the State University in Kiev, among other places.

After the war, Stalin maintained tight surveillance; everyone was potentially an enemy or a victim. An estimated one million individuals perished without a trace as "enemies of the people." Nina had learned to observe people carefully and to evaluate a room full of strangers while maintaining a calm, friendly demeanor.

For different reasons, Jackie Kennedy also learned early to keep her thoughts and feelings to herself. She was known for her ability to keep her composure, a trait in evidence throughout the heartbreaks that she endured, even before she lost her husband. Khrushchev was impressed with Jackie. In his memoirs, he writes that he found her energetic and pleasant, quick of tongue and a resourceful conversationalist. "Don't mix it up with her," he warned. "She'll cut you down to size."

Nina was no babushka and Jackie was no simple starlet, but the press judged both women chiefly on their appearances. During Khrushchev's visit to the US, the two women developed a strong relationship, communicating with ease because Nina Petrovna spoke English.

Americans who lived through the Cuban Missile Crisis, I am told, still shudder at the memory. The feeling was no different on the other side of the Iron Curtain. I remember 1962 vividly, how we were marched out of our classroom to the streets where, it seemed, our whole town was waving Soviet flags. We were told to celebrate the greatness of Nikita Khrushchev, who had averted a nuclear war with the United States by exercising statesmanship and restraint. He won a guarantee from the US, we were told, not to attack Cuba, and, in exchange, he removed the nuclear warheads from that island because they were no longer needed.

When I came home from school that day, I saw my father, who was a tailor, chuckling over a pair of pants he was ironing. "Kennedy whipped his butt and Khrushchev had to go home with his tail between his legs."

My father, despite coming from a very poor family, built a successful business through hard work and employed six other tailors in his shop. When the Communists came to power after the war, they confiscated his business and labeled him a parasite of society. Naturally, he hated the Communist regime. He often quoted, "When it rains in Moscow, we have to carry an umbrella." But I did not especially care what the truth was. I was glad that the immediate danger had passed. In the days leading up to the resolution of the crisis, my heart had pounded in fear every time I heard the sound of an airplane.

"It is insane that two men, sitting on opposite sides of the world, should be able to decide to bring an end to civilization," President Kennedy said soon after. Khrushchev put it in a way that was even more chilling: "In nuclear war, the survivors will envy the dead."

President Kennedy and Premier Khrushchev reached an agreement on the Nuclear Test Ban Treaty, with Kennedy signing the treaty on October 7, 1963.

In her last letter from the White House following her husband's death, Jackie Kennedy wrote to Premier Khrushchev: "The danger which troubled my husband was that war might start not so much by the big men as by the little ones. While big men know the need for self-control and restraint, little men are sometimes moved more by fear and pride..." Jackie concluded with the words: "I hear that Mrs. Khrushcheva had tears in her eyes when she left the US Embassy in Moscow after signing the book of mourning. Please thank her for that."

The relationship between President Kennedy and Premier Khrushchev was the start of a dialogue. But the damage caused by an assassination in Dallas along with the removal of Khrushchev by Soviet hardliners in 1964 meant that we in Czechoslovakia had to wait until 1968 for the warmth of the Prague Spring.

Did I sense a wind of change in the fall of 1967, or was I just lucky? At that time in Czechoslovakia, it was unheard of to travel abroad, let alone to a capitalist country. People in my town thought I was crazy when I applied for an exit visa to travel to England.

But it was thanks to the most important woman in my life, my mother, that I took the plunge westward. She never missed an occasion to give me a book about some faraway country. Ignorance, she insisted, breeds fear.

I knew in my heart that when the opportunity to travel came, I had to take it. Only when the Soviet tanks rolled into Prague's Wenceslas Square on August 21, 1968, and crushed the Prague Spring did I realize how important it had been for me not to waste it.

In November of 1967, the image and the strength of those two vastly different women I admired, Jackie Kennedy and Nina Petrovna, carried my spirits high even before I boarded the plane that would take me to the big, open world. Armed with a small Slovak-English dictionary, a parting gift from my brother Pavel, I was ready for the challenge.

When I landed in London, my lofty teenager's dreams awoke to the reality that although I had taken lessons in English, I did not understand spoken English. I squeezed my dictionary for comfort and visited the restroom. Right there in front of the door marked "LOO," my youthful optimism was seriously tested. In England then, to use a bathroom one had to drop a penny in a

Naive 18-year-old arrives in England

slot to open the door. But I had no money. I had a job lined up as an au pair but, at that moment, in a foreign country and unable to communicate, across the Iron Curtain from anyone I knew, I could not "spend a penny," as they say in England.

My first night at the house where I was to work was a mixture of excitement and apprehension. I curled up in my bed and waited for fatigue to overpower the adrenaline.

The next day, with the help of my dictionary, I started to learn. Fast. No lifelines, only the one I was looking at in the mirror. In time, people's conversations no longer sounded like gibberish. Words became clearer and eventually I was able to converse with ease.

Time and fate led me to a job at a solicitor's office located opposite the Marlborough Court, on Great Marlborough Street. From my perch in the office, I watched Paul McCartney entering that very court to marry Linda Eastman.

London in the early 1970s was a mixture of burned brassieres, protests against the Vietnam War, and psychedelic music. I was eighteen years old and wanted to be part of it. I shed my bra, listened to the Beatles, and for a while I put Jackie and Nina on the backseat.

Still, I looked for guidance in my past. When Valentina Tereshkova became the first woman in space, I was taught that all women in Communist countries were emancipated. But during my senior year in high school, I also learned the narrowness of the Communist conception of an emancipated woman. Not unlike my daughter and her classmates many years later in America, girls in my class were focused on prom, hairstyles, dresses, and shoes.

Makeup was not available, but to our delight, we discovered that one of the crayons we used in an art class could double as a makeup pencil. One day, I volunteered to be the guinea pig and let another girl, the best artist in the class, put liner on my eyelids during a break between lessons. My literature teacher walked into the room; she had always liked my work and said I was a talented writer. She took one look at me and told me to stand up.

"You look stupid. Go and wash your face," she said.

With time and perseverance, I mastered the English language well enough to venture into the world that surrounded me. Ten girls were selected by London's Daily Mail newspaper in a competition to discover international models. I was lucky to be one of them. But even after I saw my face looking back at me from magazines, I could not, as much as I wanted to, ignore the voice of my teacher. Had I betrayed all that I was taught?

By the time I exchanged Big Ben for the Statue of Liberty and returned to my first love, writing—a place outwardly anonymous yet in which I would bare my soul—I wondered: Who was behind the face in the magazines? That thought would bring me once again to Jackie Kennedy and Nina Petrovna. Because of the marked difference in their physical appearances, the photographs seen all over the world failed to reveal the closeness of their inner lives and similarity of their inner strength. The irony of people underestimating Jackie because of her beauty, and Nina because of her lack of it, made me realize that the way others perceived me did not change who I was, and I was able to see who was behind the photographs in those magazines.

There I found my mother, who had the audacity to believe that an eighteen-year-old girl could successfully navigate a world she knew only from books. I found a determined young girl who grew up in a hurry yet who remained a dreamer destined to write. I found a poem penned long ago by a teenager that always provided me with hope in the darkness.

Today my hair appears to match Jackie's perfectly, but under the coloring, it is as much salt-and-pepper as Nina Petrovna's in that old photograph pinned above the wooden radio. Now I have a large television on which I see the events unfolding in Ukraine. Images of destruction and cruelty bombard us as lifeless ash replaces the once beautiful cities. I tremble at the memory of Khrushchev's words following the Cuban Missile Crisis.

Nina Petrovna, who was from Ukraine, materializes in my mind and I think of Jackie, who worried about the little men moved by fear and pride, and I feel trapped in darkness. But then I look closer and I see the grit, the grace, the dignity of these women long gone.

I look up and on the TV screen I see a little boy traveling alone from Ukraine the length of Slovakia to meet up with his brother, who is a student in Bratislava, with nothing more than his brother's cellphone number written on his wrist. I focus on this story from my homeland and I see the little boy's bravery, and I see beauty in the actions of kindness he encounters on his journey. As the boy is interviewed, a little piece of blue sky is visible behind him, and I am transported back to my family's room, and a poem that once again inspires hope in me.

Jackie, Nina, and Me was published by **BioStories** in the Fall Issue, 2022.

Anika
Pavel

Height 5'7
Bust 34 Waist 24 Hips 35
Dress 12 Shoes 6½
Hair: Dark Red Eyes: Green/Brown

Gross 170
Oberweite 86 Taille 61 Hüfte 89
Kleid 40 Schuhe 39½
Haare: Dunkel Rot Augen: Grün/Braun

ACTRESS/EQUITY MEMBER

Freddies
2 Lowndes Street
London SW1
235 8778

DANGER

CLAIROL
Nice'n
Easy
CONDITIONING HAIR COLOUR
YOU JUST SHAMPOO IN

success is a loaded word

In the world of acting and modeling, fame and success are often intertwined. Because I never thought of myself as famous, I could not see my success. As I started to gather pages of my modeling work for this book, I was surprised at how much work I have done. I even found one of my old TV commercials still on line. And so, at last I came to realize that I did have a successful modeling career. Whether I will have a successful writing career will depend on you, dear reader.

acknowledgments

I have been very lucky with all my teachers. Starting in my high school, Professor Vavrova, my literature and writing teacher told me that she was more critical of my work because she believed I could do better. She also published three of my essays in our school magazine.

My first teacher in America, Cindi Myers, a successful author herself, who even after she was no longer my teacher, always found time to follow my progress, to read my work, give me advice and share my joy whenever my work got published.

My teacher at NYU, Carol Bergman, taught me that re-writing can be a pleasure if we see it the right way. Richard Bausch and Nicolas Delbanco taught classes that I have taken in Kauai at a writers' conference. I am especially thankful to Nicolas Delbanco who I learned was a fellow Cape Coder and who generously continued to give me advice, took time to read my work and became a dear and much appreciated friend. Kris Franklin started as my teacher and became an editor, advisor, friend and my cheer leader. I would have given up many times if it were not for Kris lifting me up when I felt down; he was not afraid to clip my wings when I was getting too close to the sun. Thanks Kris.

I am deeply grateful to Elizabeth Ridley for her invaluable input and her detailed mind which was so necessary for my flighty one. I am thankful for her advice and her support.

Mark Leichter the editor of bioStories was the first to publish my work and to nominate it for the Pushcart Prize. Mark is one of those rare editor/writers who selflessly helps a fellow writer no matter how busy he might be.

YJ Fischer who bravely waded through my very first efforts and always found something positive in my early rumblings.

Emma Hamilton who also saw her fair share of early misspelled efforts yet always found time to advise and help with the multiple rewrites.

Victoria Heath Silk who designed the cover and exhibited endless patience with my ever-changing mind.

I could not have done it without my marketing director Kristen O'Connell, and special thanks to my website designer Matthew Young.

I would like to thank all my friends and family who read my first efforts and who provided advice, valuable photos and always encouragement.

A very special thanks goes to my cousins Eddie and Elenka. I knew retelling Eddie's story from Korea for my essay *Still Lucky* was not easy for him. Eddie has sadly passed away but not before he was able to read the published essay in Ariel Chart the International Journal. I dedicate that essay to all Korean War veterans.

My family. I am grateful to my brothers Jan and Pavel who toughened me up when I was a kid but who were always there for me when I needed them. My nephew Matko Kocvara, a wonderful artist who has transferred my vision for the logo perfectly.

I am grateful to Palo Kocvara, my nephew, without whom the world of the internet would have never heard from me.

My children Jimmy, Danny and Helena encouraged me and fended countless calls and emails when I needed opinion or advice. Their spouses Emma, Therese, and James, who put up with the intrusion. My husband Jim, whose support sustained me in countless ways and without whom this book would never have seen the light of the day.

All the people in London who helped me survive and thrive, especially those with whom I still exchange Christmas Cards, but I have to remember more specifically my friend Carolyn Holledge who was always there for me in London and later, depending which country I was calling from, she often fended my middle of the night calls with her typical kindness and calm. I also cannot forget Katrina Schaefer who never fails to remind me that life is full of roses if we choose to see them.

I fear I forgot someone and I am sure on this journey I will come across many who will help me but at some point, the book is set and no changes can be made. To those I say, please forgive me.

Anika Pavel

photo credits

about the author

Anika Pavel was born Jarmila Kocvarova in communist Czecho-slovakia. What was intended as a one-year stay in England turned her into a refugee when the Soviet Union invaded her homeland.

Anika Pavel's writing draws from the varied experiences of her life, which has taken her to three continents, brought her across geopolitical divides, and made her a witness to many historical events.

Her essays have been published online, in print and nominated for the Pushcart Prize. www.anikapavel.com